WOODROW WILSON

Signal Corps, U.S. Army

REAR ADMIRAL CARY T. GRAYSON AND PRESIDENT WOODROW WILSON

WOODROW WILSON

An Intimate Memoir

by

REAR ADMIRAL CARY T. GRAYSON

POTOMAC BOOKS, INC. PUBLISHERS   WASHINGTON

SECOND EDITION

Library of Congress Catalog Card Number: 60-10998
International Standard Book Number: 0-87107-038-3

Printed in the United States of America

Foreword

ONE NAME that has been missing from the list of those who have told some version of the "inside story" of Woodrow Wilson is Admiral Cary T. Grayson. Grayson, the President's personal physician and naval aide, was uniquely qualified to tell such a story. From the time Wilson came to Washington, Grayson was almost constantly at his side. He saw him daily in the White House. He was with him in Paris. He accompanied him on the tour to rally the country to the League which ended in the President's collapse. With the exception of Mrs. Wilson, he was practically the only one who had access to Wilson during the first months of his convalescence. And in the last years of Wilson's life, he helped care for him in the house on S Street.

In these twelve years of intimate association, Cary Grayson came to know and understand Wilson as few men did and to know, too, much untold history. Familiarity, in this case, did not breed disillusion and disenchantment as it so often does. As the friend of both Wilson and Grayson, I know how strong was the bond between the two.

Grayson not only admired Wilson as a gifted and high-principled leader, but he was devoted to him as a warm human being. Wilson reciprocated this regard and affection. Grayson was more than his doctor helping him to husband his never robust health. He was also a discreet and able aide who could be entrusted with difficult and delicate tasks. Above all, Grayson was the loyal and understanding friend, one of the very few to whom Wilson, in the crushing loneliness of the Presidency, could unburden his innermost thoughts. A President is never at a loss for aides, advisers, assistants—even sociable companions. But he is ever in need of the intellectually compatible friend who wants nothing, who represents nobody, whom he can trust implicitly.

This described Grayson. In him Wilson found a man of keen intelligence, deep religious feelings, and a highly developed sense of duty—qualities which mirrored his own. But Grayson also had wit and charm which endeared him to Wilson as it did to everybody. The President could be gay, too, but only in the secure circle of family and friends. Grayson shared his gift of laughter with all. He was the best storyteller I ever knew. His yarns, whether about the rustic neighbors of his boyhood home in Culpeper County, Virginia, or about the world's luminaries he knew at Versailles, always poked good-natured but instructive fun at human foibles—including his own. Some of Grayson's most memorable stories were told on himself.

After Wilson's death Grayson continued active in medicine; pursued his interest in the turf; and served with conspicuous success as head of the American Red Cross, a post he accepted at the behest of his devoted friend, F.D.R. But through the years he steadfastly refused to publish anything about Wilson.

This was in character. His modesty and discretion and his regard for the private and privileged nature of his relationship to the President imposed silence on him. He did, however, keep a diary, and in 1924 set down some recollections of the human side of Woodrow Wilson, which were found among his papers on his death in 1938. These recollections are published now and they are still intensely interesting. This is not a full dress study of Woodrow Wilson; it does not deal with the *President* but the *man*. Here we have a character study which is warm, affectionate, and honest. This little book brings Woodrow Wilson alive. This is the man as I knew him.

—BERNARD BARUCH

April, 1960

Preface

I<small>T WAS MY PRIVILEGE</small> to be in constant association
with Mr. Wilson from March 3, 1913, the day before
his inauguration, until February 3, 1924, the day of
his death. At the beginning of his Administration I
was appointed Naval Aide and private physician, and
the official relationship grew rapidly into a very close
personal relationship. Not in boastfulness, but as a
statement of fact, I can say that I saw him more constantly and more intimately than any other man during those eleven years.

I heard him discuss many of the designs which have
become a part of history. I accompanied him on innumerable automobile rides, and was his most frequent companion in golf, the playing of which I had
urged upon him as a therapeutic measure, for he was
not robust when he entered the White House.

By reason of my office I was with him on all the
short trips and long journeys which he made on public business in this country, on most of his recreational
trips on the yacht *Mayflower,* and I was with him during the four voyages which he made to and fro across

the Atlantic Ocean in connection with the Peace Conference.

I lived in the White House much of the time before my marriage. I lived with him in Paris during the Conference, and again in the White House for many months following the beginning of his long illness. My good wife sometimes laughingly declared that I was only a visitor under my own roof, because of my prolonged absence with Mr. Wilson in Europe and because of the necessity of being within his call during the first seven or eight months of his illness.

He treated me as an older man might treat his son, confided to me many of his views and his opinions of public men with whom he dealt in America and abroad.

In the earlier part of his Administration, and after the death of his first wife, there were periods when he ordered his family away from the summer heat of Washington where his duties compelled him to remain, and in these times I was often his sole companion in the White House.

On automobile rides, in evening talks, sometimes long, sometimes shortened by public business, he opened his mind to me as to no one else, except his wife, not only on public matters, but on literature, which he loved dearly, and in reminiscence of past experiences, as Governor of New Jersey, as President of Princeton University, as a professor in Princeton, Wesleyan and Bryn Mawr. He talked to me about his student days in Princeton and Davidson, about his boyhood, about his family, especially his father, whose memory he revered, who had been his chief teacher, and the man of all the world whom he most admired and loved. Gayety of spirits, puns, anecdotes, limericks garnished his graver conversation, so that I became familiar with his lighter moods as well as his more weighty thoughts.

It was an extraordinary privilege to be so close to the foremost man of his age, to see him shape policies which were destined to give a new direction to men's thoughts everywhere, to see him courageously face good report and evil report, to see him welcomed in Europe as the deliverer of the world from its crushing perplexities. It was no less wonderful to see him face with equanimity after the war what many considered his repudiation by the majority of his fellow citizens, and, again, to see him reinstated in the confidence of the American people, and, in the end, to see him acknowledged everywhere as the embodiment of the loftiest spirit, the supreme mind of his generation, one of the immortals of the world's history.

It was a golden opportunity to know him intimately on his human side, that side which because of his own reserve and people's misunderstanding of him is less known than the grandeur of his public character. This book deals little with politics or with analyses of Mr. Wilson's unusual personality. It presents him through anecdote and narrative as I saw him close at hand during a critical period of American history.

CHAPTER

1

My OFFICIAL CONNECTION with Mr. Wilson was almost accidental, though, as I look back over the long stretch of years, I should like to call it providential. After the official luncheon on March 4th, 1913, Mr. Wilson's sister, Mrs. Annie Howe, fell on one of the marble staircases and cut her brow. As I was present as a guest and had my equipment handy, I sewed up the wound and attended her for a few days thereafter. The President commented on how promptly it was done and wanted to know if I was prepared for the operation before the accident occurred.

Mr. Wilson asked me to lunch one day, when one of the other guests was the Secretary of the Navy, Mr. Josephus Daniels. To my surprise Mr. Wilson turned to the Secretary and said: "There is one part of the Navy that I want to appropriate. There have been a good many applications for the position but Mrs. Wilson and I have already become acquainted with

Doctor Grayson and we have decided that he is the man we should like to have assigned to the White House." To which Secretary Daniels replied jokingly: "You generally have to come to the Navy when you want a good thing." That is all there is to the story. No official action was necessary because I had already been assigned to the White House during the Taft Administration and the assignment was simply continued.

A few days later, on a Sunday morning, I was called into professional attendance upon the President. When I entered the sickroom, Mrs. Wilson, who was standing by the bed, greeted me with her gracious smile. I found the patient lying in bed suffering from a headache and digestive disturbance, which he described as a "turmoil in Central America." He said: "When you get to know me better, you will find that I am subject to disturbances in the equatorial regions." My first professional advice was an injunction to remain in bed, in reply to which he said: "You are advising a new President, and you are giving him bad advice, for you are telling him not to go to church."

This was the beginning of my diagnosis of his general condition and my systematic treatment which depended very little upon drugs. Indeed, when I took his medicines away from him he accused me of being a "therapeutic nihilist." It seemed to me a clear case for preventive medicine. I was able to get his coöperation in my plans through a simple appeal to his reason. I reminded him that he had four hard years ahead of him and that he owed it to himself and the

American people to get into as fit condition as possible and to stay there. The regime included plenty of fresh air, a diet suited to his idiosyncrasies as I discovered them by close study, plenty of sleep, daily motor rides, occasional trips on the *Mayflower,* and especially regular games of golf, together with treatment for a persistent case of neuritis from which he had long suffered.

By reason of his outdoor recreation and exercise, I was quickly drawn into close, personal association with him, for I was his regular companion in these diversions. I learned to know something of his habits of mind and his sense of humor, which, by the way, was one of the things that assisted much in enabling me to keep him in good condition.

It was the second day of his first illness that he told me some of his characteristic anecdotes. He told me of Doctor Delafield, the New York specialist, an admirable physician but without much sense of humor, who, when he started first to wash out Mr. Wilson's stomach, stood before him with a long rubber tube in his hand and said in a very serious manner: "You will find this extremely disagreeable but not intolerable."

I soon learned that it was easy to get to know Mr. Wilson—if he happened to take a fancy to you. Contrary to widespread opinion, he was not temperamentally cold. He was austere in his public relationships. He would not allow friendship to influence his course of duty. Several years later he told me that if he had a son who was convicted on a criminal charge, and whose case should come before him as Chief Executive, he would confirm the judgment of the court and then die of a broken heart.

Hence he was sometimes called aloof and was sometimes taxed with ingratitude. Professional politicians who placed rewards and patronage above political ethics could not understand Mr. Wilson's impersonal attitude in politics. Richard Croker's summarization of him has become famous—"An ingrate is no good in politics." The former New York boss had in mind Governor-elect Wilson's opposition to the candidacy of former Senator James Smith, Jr., of New Jersey, for reëlection to the United States Senate. Neither Senator Smith nor Mr. Croker could understand the mind and actions of a man who placed principle above everything else, even rewards to those who, like Senator Smith, had assisted him into office.

It required courage of a rare sort to oppose Senator Smith's ambition. Mr. Wilson had told Senator Smith and other members of the committee who proposed to nominate him for the Governorship of New Jersey that he could accept the nomination only on the condition that it put him under obligations to no individual but left him free in each instance to act in accordance with what he conceived to be the best interests of the people of New Jersey at large.

When the Democratic State Primary selected James E. Martine for senator, Mr. Wilson stood on the principle that a primary election choice must be respected, that the question of personality was insignificant as compared with keeping faith with the people's choice. On that principle he must stand though he knew he would be charged with ingratitude.

Woodrow Wilson was never afraid of being misunderstood when a principle which he held inviolable was involved. He was not callous. He was sensitive as literary men usually are. In his address at the services held in the Brooklyn Navy Yard in memory of those who lost their lives in the expedition to Vera Cruz in 1914, there occurred this significant passage:

> I never went into battle; I was never under fire; but I fancy that there are some things just as hard to do as to go under fire. I fancy that it is just as hard to do your duty when men are sneering at you as when they are shooting at you. When they shoot at you, they can only take your natural life; when they sneer at you, they can wound your living heart, and men who are brave enough, steadfast enough, steady in their principles enough, to go about their duty with regard to their fellowmen, no matter whether there are hisses or cheers . . . are men for a nation to be proud of. . . . The cheers of the moment are not what a man ought to think about, but the verdict of his conscience and of the consciences of mankind.

Consciously or unconsciously Woodrow Wilson made there a better analysis of his motives for action than anybody else can make. He was sincere in his principles, and he had the courage to stand for them in the face of all consequences. He broke with some of his friends, and the breaks hurt him, but these severances were due to differences on some matter of principle. He was impersonal in the sense that he would not and could not allow a friendship to stand between him and what he conceived to be his public duty.

Much has been written and will be written about his quarrels, and it has sometimes been asserted that he had no personal friends. They who say this ignore the record. For many old Princeton classmates and collegemates he kept a romantic affection to the end of his life. There were Cyrus McCormick, Cleveland Dodge, Robert Bridges, E.P. Davis, Edward Sheldon, Charles Talcott, the brothers Thomas and David Jones. There were associates in the Princeton faculty like Harry Fine, John Westcott, George Harper, Winthrop Daniels, Edward Capps. There were political associates, including members of his Cabinet, between whom and him there was not only no break in official relationships, but an affection which endured to his life's end: Newton Baker, Josephus Daniels, Thomas W. Gregory, David F. Houston, Carter Glass, William B. Wilson. There were many Members of Congress, including John Sharp Williams, Claude A. Swanson, Cordell Hull, Finis Garrett. There were men whom he had appointed to diplomatic positions, like Thomas Nelson Page, Henry Morgenthau, Roland S. Morris, Pleasant Stovall (a school-boy friend), and Charles R. Crane. There were members of special war agencies such as Norman Davis, Bernard

Baruch, Frank L. Polk, Vance McCormick, Jesse H. Jones.

These are merely outstanding figures among many for whom Mr. Wilson retained to the end a warm, positive friendship. Many of them were frequent visitors to the house in S Street throughout the period of Mr. Wilson's retirement. They called unostentatiously, unofficially, as personal friends.

By nature Mr. Wilson was kind, considerate, and extraordinarily thoughtful—qualities illustrated by a little episode in Los Angeles in September, 1919. He had been through a terrible ordeal of public speaking while seriously ill, had been obliged to respond to the greetings of hundreds and thousands along the line of travel, had been suffering from insomnia and an attack of asthma, was unable to digest his food, and was in a condition which caused me serious apprehension. The day before he arrived in Los Angeles he had spoken twice in San Diego, once in the stadium to an outdoor audience of fifty thousand people, which he had to address by megabox. He told me that it was the most difficult speech he had ever made in his life because he felt he was speaking artificially through a mechanical contrivance.

In Los Angeles he spoke twice—once to an audience of fifteen thousand people. His physical and nervous condition would certainly have justified him in declining any additional effort even to gratify his most intimate personal friends. But someone casually mentioned to him that he or she was acquainted with Mrs.

Janie Porter Candler. The President replied: "Oh, yes, Mrs. Candler was a very dear friend of my first wife," and immediately made arrangements to call on her. She and her sister, Mrs. Hardin, were living with their families in a cottage in inconspicuous Thompson Street, far away from the center of the city. The President and Mrs. Wilson drove to Thompson Street and had one of the secret service men inquire for the house. They met Mrs. Hardin and some of the children of the younger generation, but Mrs. Candler and another sister, Miss Porter, had gone to the train to catch a glimpse of the President. When Mr. Wilson learned of this he told Mrs. Hardin that he would have the secret service men find Mrs. Candler at the station. Mrs. Candler was a little startled when she found herself being sought by the police at the railway station. She boarded the train and had a visit with the President and Mrs. Wilson.

The episode illustrates the kindness not only of President Wilson but of Mrs. Wilson. The episode illustrates another quality of President Wilson—his aversion to making publicity material out of his human qualities. Here was an occasion for a newspaper hearthrob: The foremost man of the Nation on the most important errand of his whole career, making a fight for the League of Nations against the compact and growing opposition of Congress, spending sleepless nights, exhausting days, working himself to the last remnants of his vitality, turning aside to visit a family who had upon him only the human claim that they had been friends of his dead wife; and his living wife, with that beauty of nature so characteristic of her, going with him to pay the tribute. Here was something out of which to make a newspaper story which would offset the charges which were being brought against him daily—that he was a cold man without human instincts. And yet this episode went practically unnoticed in the daily press. Almost any other public man in the circumstances would have seen to it that the newspapermen got this story.

His approach to most public men was courteous but not often familiar, and yet no one knew better how to lighten a serious interview with humorous repartee or anecdote. He was by nature dignified but assumed no artificial dignity. He told me with glee how in the gubernatorial campaign in New Jersey an old farmer slapped him on the back at the conclusion of a speech and said: "Doc, you are all right." The President added: "I knew then that I had arrived as a politician."

He was impatient with pompous people and intolerant of those who sought special favors from the Government. And because he cherished privacy more than display, he gave his full confidence to comparatively few, and those chiefly of his own household, of which it was my good fortune to become promptly an adopted member.

I think he appreciated the fact that I consistently refused pressure from outside to be a go-between, and that I confined my advice to matters of health, to

which he listened attentively and followed unques-
tioningly. He did me the honor to assume that I knew
what I was talking about, and, therefore, did not
argue with me.

Occasionally he himself asked me to attend to a
political matter for him, but the cases were very few
in which I voluntarily offered any political advice,
and when I did it was on some personal ground. What
I mean by this can be illustrated by an incident concerning the son of Mr. Lawrence Washington, the last
relative of George Washington to be born at Mount
Vernon. I found that Mr. Washington had a son
whom he was very anxious to have appointed to West
Point, and as he was a resident of the District of
Columbia there was no very direct way of approach to
this end. Having no political "pull" he was unsuccess-
ful through Senators and Congressmen. I therefore
took my courage in my hands and went to the President and asked him to make an exception to the rule
of appointing to the Military Academy a youth who
was not the son of an officer in any of the services. The
President said: "I cannot consider it. I will not break
the rule." "But, Mr. President," I said, "this is an
unusual case. It is in the name of George Washington
that I am asking you to break the rule." Whereupon
I stated the case to him and he replied: "Well, if it is
for George I cannot refuse. Go over to Secretary
Garrison, state the case to him, and I am sure he will
agree with me." The young man was appointed to
West Point.

My personal acquaintanceship and friendship with Mr. Wilson grew simultaneously with my professional knowledge of his physical constitution. He often expressed to me his views as one muses aloud, finding in me a safety valve.

He was never happier than in the bosom of his family, sitting before the fireplace in the Oval Room with us, chatting comfortably. Sometimes his conversation was playful, at other times serious. He would pun, recite nonsense verse and limericks, and then suddenly turn from merriment to gravity, frequently referring to or reading some passage from Burke or Bagehot, from which he would be likely to pass to an essay by Charles Lamb, or Birrell, or Chesterton (in whose glittering paradoxes he found expressed a good deal of his own philosophy of progressive conservatism), or to one of the poets whom he loved, Wordsworth (his favorite), or Browning (a few of whose poems he cherished deeply), or to the poetry of Matthew Arnold, for whose prose he did not care very much.

He was fond of reading aloud in modulated tones from his favorite authors. On the library table close at hand for reference was a copy of Burton Stevenson's large anthology of verse, from which he would sometimes read John Burroughs' poem "Waiting," finding in it perhaps a philosophy of his own life. "For, lo! my own shall come to me," as it did come before his death, after all the fluctuations of rejection and acceptance by the world's opinion. Then from the same book he would read from Lear's nonsense verse and W.S. Gilbert's swinging lyrics—he was especially fond of the Duke of Plaza-Tora.

Occasionally he and his daughter Margaret would sing together a varied repertoire: sometimes old-fashioned Southern songs, sometimes lyrics of Gilbert, or "Old Nassau," the Princeton song, and, especially on Sunday evenings, some of his favorite hymns—"The Day is Dying in the West," "The Son of God Goes Forth to War," "How Firm a Foundation," "The Strife of Life Is O'er."

He had no craving for novelty but liked to do the same thing over and over again. He reread the same books, repeated the same automobile rides, as also, before he came into the Presidency, he revisited many times the English lake country, which he preferred to other parts of Great Britain or to the European Continent.

He had strong attachments for articles of long association. He was particularly fond of an old cape and an old gray sweater, which he had purchased in Scotland on one of his bicycling tours in his young manhood, and to which he clung to the end of his life. Handsome sweaters were sent to him as presents, and occasionally he would wear one of them, but would invariably return to his old friend, the Scottish gray sweater with a moth hole in it. It traveled with him wherever he went. It was part of his luggage in Buckingham Palace, in the Quirinal, in the Royal Palace in Brussels. When he was ill in the White House he wore it in bed on all occasions, even when he received the King and Queen of the Belgians and the Prince of Wales. He wore it on his last automobile ride.

In a similar way he clung to a favorite walking stick. He had literally hundreds of canes, some of them purchased when he was a young man, many more of them given to him by friends and admirers after he had become famous. But after he was stricken, he selected one which he always referred to as his "third leg," and he would use no other.

He was preëminently a man of habit—of good habits. He had been taught in childhood not to take more food on his plate than he wanted to eat, and this became a lifelong practice. Once when I remarked on this habit of his, he laughingly said that it was part of his thrifty Scotch training.

CHAPTER

2

HE ALWAYS ATTENDED Sunday morning service at the Central Presbyterian Church, located when he came to Washington at Third and I Streets, Northwest, and subsequently removed to a new building at Sixteenth and Irving Streets. He made an address at the laying of the foundation stone of the new edifice, and he and his wife had a keen satisfaction in watching the progress of the building, of which the Reverend Doctor James H. Taylor was pastor.

Mr. Wilson was a lover of sermons if they were sincere and thoughtful, and often as he would ride down Sixteenth Street from the church he would express his admiration for the way in which Doctor Taylor had developed his subject.

It was characteristic of the President to unite with a modest congregation rather than with one of the more fashionable Presbyterian churches of Washington.

He attended church as unostentatiously as the most humble worshipers in the Capital. He was the son of a Presbyterian preacher and went to church in the spirit of worship and not for display. He could not have been distinguished from any other devout churchgoer except for the facts that he rode in a car blazoned with the President's seal and was followed, as the law required, by secret service men.

When the war began and his family had grown smaller (Miss Jessie had married Mr. Sayre and moved to New England, Miss Eleanor had married Mr. McAdoo and united with another church), there was usually room in his pew for others, and Mr. Wilson requested that doughboys occupy the pew with him.

He joined reverently in the prayers and heartily in the singing of the hymns, sometimes sharing his hymnbook with a stranger, sometimes crossing the aisle to give it to others. Knowing most of the hymns by memory he was able to continue singing without the book.

Once he absented himself from state duties to attend a meeting of the Presbytery in the Central Presbyterian Church, where he made an address, speaking with authority because he was a ruling elder in the Presbyterian Church.

Wherever he was he attended divine services—in whatever town he might be spending a Sunday on one of his official trips, in Cornish, New Hampshire, and at Shadow Lawn in New Jersey (where he took the brief vacations he had during his terms as President), on shipboard, and at the Paris Conference.

A memorable church service which President Wilson attended, and in which he involuntarily shared, was at Carlisle, England, in 1918. He had participated in many formal functions on the Continent and in Great Britain preparatory to the opening of the Peace Conference in Paris, but he made a special request that on December 29th he might be free of official formalities in order to visit and worship in the Presbyterian Church at Carlisle, where his grandfather, the Reverend Thomas Woodrow, had been pastor, and where his mother had gone to church as a little girl. So notable a visitor could not have his wishes for privacy entirely gratified. Arriving in Carlisle in a heavy rainstorm, he and Mrs. Wilson were officially received by the city dignitaries and other officials, ecclesiastical and military, with most of the populace as onlookers. There was a reception at the Crown and Mitre Hotel, where he was shown documents pertaining to his father. Here he posed with Thomas Watson, ninety years of age, who had been a member of Dr. Woodrow's Sunday School class. The photographer set off a flash light, which startled the old man, and he turned and clutched the President by the arm. Then apparently realizing what it had meant he whispered in the President's ear, and the President nodded, and then told the photographers to take another flash. It developed later that the old man had said to the President: "Can't we take another? I am sure I blinked that time, and the picture won't be good. I want a good picture in your honor."

Our party visited the compact brick house in which the President's mother was born, and then proceeded to the church, which was crowded. Mr. and Mrs. Wilson were assigned to conspicuous seats and participated in the service. After the sermon, the pastor, contrary to Mr. Wilson's request, asked him to say a few words to the congregation. Though taken unawares, the President made an eloquent, brief address, which deeply touched everyone present:

It is with unaffected reluctance that I project myself into this solemn service. I remember my grandfather very well, and, remembering him as I do, I am confident that he would not approve of it. I remember how much he required. I remember the stern lessons of duty he gave me. I remember also, painfully, the things which he expected me to know which I did not know. I know there has come a change of times when a layman like myself is permitted to speak in a congregation. But I was reluctant because the feelings that have been excited in me are too intimate and too deep to permit of public expression. The memories that have come to me today of the mother who was born here are very affecting; and her quiet character, her sense of duty, and dislike of ostentation have come back to me with increasing force as those years of duty have accumulated.

Yet perhaps it is appropriate that in a place of worship I should acknowledge my indebtedness to her and her remarkable father, because, after all, what the world is now seeking to do is to return to the paths of duty, to turn away from the savagery of interest to the dignity of the performance of right. And I believe that as this war has drawn the nations tem-

porarily together in a combination of physical force
we shall now be drawn together in a combination of
moral force that will be irresistible.

It is moral force that is irresistible. It is moral force
as much as physical that has defeated the effort to
subdue the world. Words have cut as deep as the
sword. The knowledge that wrong was being at-
tempted has aroused the nations. They have gone out
like men upon a crusade. No other cause could have
drawn so many nations together. They knew that an
outlaw was abroad who purposed unspeakable
things. It is from quiet places like this all over the
world that the forces accumulate which presently will
overbear any attempt to accomplish evil on a large
scale. Like the rivulets gathering into the river and
the river into the sea, there come from communities
like this streams that fertilize the consciences of men,
and it is the conscience of the world that we are
trying to place upon the throne which others would
usurp.

This was not Mr. Wilson's first visit to his grandfather's church. Years before as a professorial tourist
he had ventured into the church one Sunday morning
clad in bicycle costume, the only clothes he had with
him, and nothing to denote that he was a Presbyterian
elder. He was admitted doubtfully by a verger, who
was a stickler for form, and shown to a pew in a
remote corner. The President contrasted the two
visits, remarking that the difference between them
was "somewhat noticeable."

In Paris, the Reverend Doctor Hugh Black, whom
Mr. Wilson had often heard in Edinburgh and in

America, was to preach, and at the conference on the preceding Saturday Mr. Wilson told Mr. Lloyd George and M. Clemenceau that he was going to hear a great preacher the next day, and invited them to join him. M. Clemenceau declined on the score that he had never been inside of a church, and he did not propose to spoil his record so late in life. Mr. and Mrs. Wilson attended the service, as did Mr. Lloyd George, and the latter agreed with Mr. Wilson that they had heard a great sermon.

Apology is unnecessary for detailed accounts of Mr. Wilson's relationship with the church, because religion was flesh of his flesh and bone of his bone. He kept the faith which he inherited from his fore-fathers. He was deeply religious outside of church and on weekdays, as well as inside and on Sundays.

Though he loved anecdotes, he shrank away from any that carried the slightest suggestion of sacrilege. In the first year of daylight saving time, someone re-peated in his presence the story of the old Virginia cook who was told to have dinner ready at seven o'clock, and answered irritably: "By what time—Wilson's time or Christ's time?" Everybody in the group laughed, and for a moment Mr. Wilson's own face broke into a smile over the absurdity, but he quickly strangled the smile and remarked: "That is irreverent."

He was no maudlin pietist. He was too much a man for that, and he could laugh, as did his preacher father, at anecdotes about preachers.

He was fond of repeating one of his father's stories of a Scotch dominie who prayed at length, giving the Lord much information, and concluded with: "And Oh Lord, there is much more of this matter, as Thou hast doubtless read in the last number of the Edinburgh *Review*."

CHAPTER

3

AFTER A WHILE, I became convinced that an occasional evening at the theatre would be beneficial to him. He had never been a regular theatre-goer, and I had difficulty in making this a part of his new regime. At last he consented, and once a week he and Mrs. Wilson and I, sometimes with guests, attended a play.

It was like him to settle down after a little to Poli's, where a stock company was then playing, rather than to experiment with the visiting companies at the National and Belasco's, because in describing Woodrow Wilson one cannot too often emphasize his preference for doing the same thing repeatedly. Like the President, Captain W.E. Luckett, his wife, and his mother-in-law were weekly attendants at Poli's, occupying seats in the front row of the gallery. The old steamboat captain, one of the best known in Potomac River and Chesapeake Bay navigation, being a true philosopher, had retired while there was still time to enjoy life and to cultivate his little garden: "I have accumulated enough for comfort; why should I want more?" The captain, who was a staunch follower of Mr. Wilson, was always in his seat when the Presidential party arrived. As Mr. Wilson entered his box two or three minutes before it was time for the performance to begin, for he had "the King's virtue, promptness," Captain Luckett would rise and stand, the President would turn to the gallery, and the two would salute each other. The audience would cheer and a moment later the curtain would be rung up.

However, after the Poli stock company had been disbanded, Mr. Wilson would occasionally appear in a box at one of the other houses. He did this especially during the war in recognition of the necessity of diversion from the problems which were pressing upon him and the momentous daily decisions upon which hung the destinies of nations. His theatrical tastes were catholic, that is to say, he would watch a serious drama with discriminating criticism, but he would also laugh at nonsense comedy and enjoy a melodious musical show.

His favorite comedian was Will Rogers, and his laughter at the comedian's jokes at the expense of the Administration was spontaneous and hearty. Two weeks after the President's death Mr. Rogers' weekly newspaper syndicate letter was a touching tribute to Mr. Wilson with some reminiscences of the actor's experience in performing on the stage before an audience which included the Chief Magistrate. Mr. Rogers said that on his first appearance before Mr.

Wilson he was badly frightened, but that when he gave a "crack" at the Administration and saw the President chuckling with amusement, he was encouraged to bolder utterances. That night Mr. Wilson showed his good sportsmanship by going backstage to shake hands with the comedian and chat with him. Mr. Rogers' article mingled pathos with humor and concluded thus: "The world lost a friend. The theatre lost its greatest supporter. And I lost the most distinguished person who has laughed at my little nonsensical jokes. . . . Now I have only to look back on him as my greatest memory."

The joke which, according to Mr. Rogers, "took best" and was often repeated by Mr. Wilson to his friends was that the President was "five notes behind" in his correspondence with Germany. This was before the United States entered the war.

Some of Mr. Wilson's guests in a box party recalled another Rogers' joke which caught the President's fancy: "I see the President has written another note," said Rogers, as he twirled his lariat, and, after a moment's pause, in his Western drawl, he added, "The President must have a hard time making both the high-brows and the boneheads understand what he means." "He is right," the President whispered to a friend who sat nearby.

In Paris Mr. Wilson had little time to attend the theatre, nor did he care for the usual type of French comedy. But in the spring of 1919 he saw an English company in a clean variety show which entertained him so much that he went a second time. At this second performance an impromptu incident occurred, which Mr. Wilson several times related with amusement. On a table set in the center of the stage was piled a number of chairs and, topping all, a ladder; a cockney holding a banjo in one hand climbed to the giddy top of the teetering structure, balanced himself, and asked the audience to name tunes which they would like to hear played. In response to the invitation a voice from the audience called out, "Nearer My God to Thee." Whether or not it was a "plant," it was carried through with such verisimilitude that the man on the dizzy height seemed visibly embarrassed and even a little frightened by the fearsome implication.

During Mr. Wilson's second administration and later, after his retirement to private life, he was a weekly attendant on Saturday nights at Keith's in Washington. Mr. Robbins, the manager, made every provision for his comfort when he was an invalid. Mr. Wilson's car would drive through waiting throngs into an alley, he would be helped out by Scott, the faithful negro valet, and into one of the seats reserved for him and Mrs. Wilson and their party at the rear of the house only a few steps from the entrance door.

On Saturday nights rear seats were in demand, and the ticket sellers would say: "This is as near to him as I can place you," it being unnecessary to specify to whom "him" referred.

When the performance was over the actors would throng the narrow alley and applaud as he laboriously climbed back into his car. Sometimes an actress would step forward respectfully and hand to him a huge spray of flowers purchased by the performers. "We simply want to tell you that we love you dearly," was the graceful remark of one of these spokeswomen one evening. Then the automobile would back out of the alley and make its way carefully through the thousands of spectators who jammed G Street.

During his illness he sometimes invited a few friends to his home to see a motion picture, the film and the operator provided by Mr. Long of the Rialto motion picture house.

The homage of players and playgoers was unsolicited by Mr. Wilson, whose acquired fondness for the theatre was unostentatious. The warmhearted theatre folk felt that in him they had a quiet, silent friend, and it is remarkable how well they understood his aversion to being exploited. Few ever used his attendance as a means of advertisement.

The crowds in G Street, which grew from year to year and from month to month, were a symbol of the increasing love of the American people for one who had practically given his life for the greatest cause on earth—peace and human happiness. He was probably loved more after he retired from the Presidency than at any time during his occupation of the great office. All over the land his face or figure flashed upon the screen was a signal for tumultuous applause. No active officeholder received such demonstrations from theatrical audiences as this private citizen, who, having given everything he had to the cause of humanity, retired into dignified silence.

Because it was necessary to conserve his strength he was compelled to deny himself to general visitors, but thousands every year called at the front door to leave their cards as tokens of respect and good will—American public men, foreign diplomats, private citizens, including some of the actors who had learned to love him across the footlights. Whenever Will Rogers played in Washington he would visit the S Street house and leave some such message as: "I am not asking to see him. Just tell him that I love him."

CHAPTER

4

THE TRAGEDIES OF MR. WILSON'S life developed in
rapid succession. After a little over seventeen months
in the White House the first Mrs. Wilson died. She
was gentle but strong, quiet in her tastes, but faithful
in her obligations as the lady of the White House, performing her duties there as she had conscientiously
performed them through all her life. With natural
grace of manner she presided at state dinners, but was
happiest when the company at table consisted of a
few old-time and proven friends. Her idol was her
husband. She was one of the wisest of mothers, and
one of the most loyal of friends, continually bringing
to the White House old-time friends of her husband
and herself with genuine unaffected hospitality. She
brought to Washington her old tastes and preference
for books and for art, and would occasionally slip
quietly out of the house to enjoy, unobserved, the
literary and pictorial treasures of the Congressional
Library. She also maintained her lifelong interest in

the welfare of the unfortunate, not as a professional reformer but as one anxious to help those in genuine need of help. Shortly after her arrival in Washington she became interested in the deplorable conditions of the alley life of the city, and in her unobtrusive way made personal investigations. At her instigation the President appointed a commission to survey the situation and make recommendations for the solution of the problem.

Politicians said that her intuitive political judgment was remarkably sound—it was she who persuaded her husband not to send the message advised by some of Mr. Wilson's political supporters withdrawing his name from the Baltimore Convention at a critical moment. She did not crave great place for herself, but she believed in her husband as the greatest man of his time, and for his sake she was ambitious.

Probably the only direct political request that she made of him when he was President was that he appoint an old friend of the family as Postmaster at Rome, Georgia, her girlhood home. The President called that "Ellen's appointment."

Neither she nor the President was entirely well when they moved into the White House, and the Christmas of 1913 at Pass Christian was the result of an innocent intrigue on the part of each for the other's benefit, I acting as go-between and urging each for the other's sake to take a brief winter holiday in the pleasant Gulf country.

The result was that all of us journeyed down to the Mississippi resort. Senator John Sharp Williams had represented Pass Christian as an ideal winter resort and his motion was enthusiastically seconded by Representative (later Senator) Pat Harrison, who, in answer to my inquiries, informed me that there was a fine golf course there—not many natural hazards but "well built up."

The President of necessity took his work and his responsibilities with him, and one stormy night he sailed out into the Gulf to meet and confer with the Honorable John Lind, special representative to Mexico, for at that time the turbulent Republic was in the throes of one of its worst revolutions and American citizens were being subjected to losses and inconveniences. A declaration of war would have been the easiest solution of the problem but two principles governed President Wilson: firstly, that he must consider all the people of the United States, and not an interested few, before taking such a momentous step, and, secondly, that he believed that each country should be given the utmost opportunity to work out its own internal problems.

Contrary to the opinions of many who prided themselves on their practicality, President Wilson believed that the Mexicans should be given the fullest opportunity to devise plans of self-government, for to him self-government meant the satisfaction of the deepest innate aspirations of any people in whatsoever part of the world they might be living.

Subsequent conduct showed that he could and would draw the sword when the rights of Americans on our side of the border were violated, but the pressure to plunge our country into war which came to him from numbers of Americans who had made investments in Mexico once caused him to say: "I sometimes have to pause and remind myself that I am President of the whole United States and not merely of a few property holders in the Republic of Mexico."

On another occasion one of this interested minority was violently urging upon him the proposition that nothing but war could settle the Mexican problem, and the President said: "I happen to know that you have two sons. If I take steps to mobilize the young of America for a Mexican war, will you promise me that your sons will be among the first to enlist?"

When he finally felt compelled to send some United States ships to Vera Cruz in 1914, as a result of which some American Marines were killed, the President was deeply depressed: "The thought haunts me that it was I who ordered those young men to their deaths," he said to me.

Amusing incidents mingled with serious events in Mississippi. One day while the President and I were returning to Pass Christian from Gulfport where we had been playing golf, a little boy about ten years of age stood in the middle of the road, and with the motions of a traffic cop, waved our automobile to a stop. It turned out that he had some oranges which he wanted to give the President. The President accepted the humble offering with thanks, asked the boy where he lived, told him to climb into the car, and drove the child to his home. The next day the President wrote him a nice letter of appreciation. A few days afterward while coming along this road the little boy waved us down again. He did not have a basket this time, but he told the President that he enjoyed the letter so much that he would like to have the President write him every week after he got back to Washington. The President was very much pleased over this little incident.

His interest in children was frequently manifested. My own little son, Gordon, was constantly in the companionship of the President during the months of his illness in the White House, and the President would hold Gordon's hand while being wheeled into the East Room to witness a motion picture.

Down in Pass Christian we were returning another day from the golf course when he noticed smoke curling up from the roof of a residence. We ran to the door and knocked and were received by the lady of the house with flutterings of excitement. "Oh, Mr. President," she exclaimed, "it is so good of you to call on me. Won't you please walk into the parlor and sit down?" To which the President replied: "I haven't time to sit down—your house is on fire."

We formed a bucket brigade but the lady in her double excitement was so confused that she seized a pitcher without any water in it. Climbing through the garret to the roof we extinguished the fire and in recognition of our prowess both the President and I were elected members of the Pass Christian Fire Department.

As a matter of course the President attended church each Sunday in Pass Christian, and on the first Sunday of our attendance the old pastor remarked: "This is the second greatest honor that ever came into my life." He did not specify what was the first but my curiosity prompted me to make special inquiry on that point, to which he replied that once President Grant had attended services in the church in which he preached. Mr. Wilson had noticed during the sermon that the hymnal was similar to the kind he used when he was a boy. Thereupon I asked the minister and he gave me a copy of the hymnal which was in good condition, except that one side of the back was gone. It was from the ancient hymnal that the President afterwards sang on Sunday evenings in the Oval Room of the White House, where the family gathered.

Mr. and Mrs. Wilson seemed to be benefited by the outing and returned to Washington "in fine fettle," to use one of the President's own favorite expressions.

But in the following spring Mrs. Wilson again showed signs of debility. As my uneasiness about her condition increased I felt it necessary to inform the President. The strain on him was hard; solicitude for his best loved one piled on top of the enormous labors of getting enacted into laws one of the most constructive legislative programs in the history of the country.

Meanwhile, Mrs. Wilson's thoughts were centered on him, not on her own illness, and she would urge me to get him out regularly for golf and automobile rides. Often she herself would admonish him, and sometimes at the dinner table he would say: "Doctor, are you free to go with me to the theatre tonight? I haven't the heart for it but Ellen insists that I must go, that nothing can make her well except the knowledge that I am keeping well, and she is a great believer in your regime of exercise and recreation."

As her illness increased he formed the habit of rising about three o'clock in the morning and slipping quietly into the sickroom to see for himself how the patient was resting. After breakfast the following morning I would find him at his desk in his private office, and he would always look up and ask the same question: "How is she, Doctor?"

"I am sorry to say, Mr. President, that I cannot report any improvement," for he wanted the truth, not false consolations. He would shake his head silently and sadly and often sigh deeply. My own anxiety was double, for her, the invalid, and for the effect of her illness upon the President.

In July Mrs. Wilson's condition grew so much worse that I brought into consultation Dr. Francis X. Dercum and Dr. E.P. Davis of Philadelphia, and Dr. Thomas R. Brown of Baltimore, who confirmed my diagnosis and my hopelessness of the patient's recovery. It was Bright's disease with complications.

It was then my duty to report the tragic prognosis

to the President. I found him in his office. He listened silently, and then with a look of anguish he said abruptly: "Let's get out of here." We walked slowly together about the grounds in the rear of the White House, saying little, for there was not much to say. After a while we sat on a bench under a tree. "What am I to do!" he exclaimed. Then bracing himself, he added: "We must be brave for Ellen's sake." He then arose and went straight to her room and remained by her bedside alone for an hour.

During the days that followed, he was by her bedside all the while when public business did not compel him to be in his office. Sometimes he held her hand in both of his, patting it gently, and half whispering at intervals the one word, "Dearie."

At times he would close one hand around hers and write shorthand memoranda for public business with the other. It was at her bedside that he wrote the note in which he offered the services of the United States to the countries of Europe in bringing about a settlement of the difficulties which were rapidly leading to the Great War.

Afterwards he told me that it was the influence of her spirit which gave him his strongest inducement to work for the peace and happiness of humanity.

On August 6, 1914, I was sitting alone with Mrs. Wilson, well aware that her life was ebbing. So was she. There had been intervals of stupor and semiconsciousness, but her mind was quite clear at that moment, though the body was very weak. Feebly she took my hand and drawing me to her, whispered: "Please take good care of Woodrow, Doctor."

A few minutes later I knew the time had come to summon the family. The President sat by her bedside, quiet, controlled, but his face drawn. When the end came peacefully, he gently folded her hands across her breast, walked to the window, and broke down, sobbing like a child.

The body was taken to Rome, Georgia, and interred in the hillside cemetery by her father and mother. During the long journey in the private car he seldom left the casket but got little broken naps on the lounge in the compartment.

On the journey back to Washington he talked constantly of her to his daughters and friends. One day he and I were alone in a compartment of the car and he spoke at length of their early days, going back to his childhood and her babyhood, and recalling how his family were visiting her family in Rome, Georgia, and how, when inquiry was made as to where he was, someone reported that he was with the baby. He added that while, of course, he did not know it then, he was probably already in love with her.

The days of widowerhood that followed were heartbreaking. The Great War was on and he had to give much thought to that, as well as to American affairs, but anyone who was with him constantly could see that there was an undercurrent of thought which had to do neither with the war nor with American public policies, but with her who had been his companion for twenty-nine years.

Because of his consideration for his daughters he insisted that Miss Margaret and Mrs. Sayre should go to the summer home at Cornish, New Hampshire, for recuperation. Against their wishes and strong protests, they felt at least compelled to comply with his will. Mrs. McAdoo, who remained with her husband in Washington, and other relatives sought to give such comfort as they could. But there were long stretches when he and I alone occupied the great house. We would meet at mealtimes and often eat alone. In the evening in the private study in the White House, I would frequently sit reading on one side of the table while he worked on the other side. When he had finished his work we would fall into conversation. He loved to talk about his childhood, boyhood, young manhood, and especially his married life. He once remarked that Mrs. Wilson had been his best literary critic, that often she would suggest the insertion of a passage in one of his public addresses, and, said he: "That was the passage which made the strongest impression upon the audience."

On another occasion he said: "I sometimes feel that the Presidency has had to be paid for with Ellen's life; that she would be living today if we had continued in the old simple life at Princeton."

Mrs. Wilson had been with him through a prolonged strain and had been wounded by every bolt which men or destiny had aimed at him. She had gone through hard years of fighting alongside him in the Princeton controversies, had seen him break in health several times, and had been his chief counselor in the events leading to the Governorship of New Jersey, and even to the Presidency. These things take their toll from a human constitution.

He talked of his old father, Doctor Joseph Wilson, whom he had loved devotedly, and whom, to the day of his own death, he regarded as a greater man than himself, saying, without any assumption of modesty, that his father had won less fame than he because he had never had so great a stage on which to perform. He talked of his gentle mother and her abiding influence and of many intimate family affairs.

He sometimes mingled lighter anecdote with these reminiscences. For instance, he told me of his greatest financial crisis when he was a student in Princeton. He had spent his last allowance and would not receive another for some time, and he did not even have money to buy a stamp to write to his father for more money. But he remembered that some time before he had dropped a penny somewhere in the room. So he moved the furniture about, found the penny back of the bureau, purchased a postal card, wrote to his father, and, until the money arrived, he was entirely without funds, being too proud to apply to any of his friends for a loan. He said: "I never had much money, but this was the one time in my life when I was literally without a cent."

CHAPTER

5

In these intimate talks he opened his mind about American public affairs and the Great War. He revealed what he could not make known to the public, his faith that the Allies were fighting for the old cause of freedom but that America's wisest present position was neutrality, and, moreover, that the American people were not ready in mind to participate in a foreign war. By logic rather than by instinct he was a sincere upholder of American neutrality. His thoughts were continually shaping themselves about the sort of peace which must follow the cessation of war, a peace founded on a compact of nations which would make future war either impossible or unlikely.

He read to me many letters of advice and reproach from American correspondents. He read to me letters from eminent men in public life, and, especially, and most memorably, the letters from Ambassador Walter Hines Page about the situation in England and the personalities whom he encountered there and the different points of view which he heard expressed. They were wonderful letters and Mr. Wilson said that Mr. Page was the best letter-writer he knew, to which he added, by the way, that President Alderman of the University of Virginia was the most eloquent public speaker that he knew.

During his first summer in the White House, when the family were in Cornish, he wrote daily to Mrs. Wilson. He did this, usually, in the evening, before we started on our automobile ride through Rock Creek Park to get cooled off before going to bed. He found time to write personal letters to friends and would sometimes read me extracts from what he had written. I recall a passage from one letter about Mr. McAdoo, after he and Miss Eleanor had become engaged to be married, in which the President gave a flattering account of his prospective son-in-law to a correspondent who had never met Mr. McAdoo. He would read from his letters descriptions of public men, favorable and unfavorable—paragraphs that would have made spicy reading in the morning newspapers. Personal letter-writing gratified his desire for self-expression, and also gave him relief after the day's business. He liked to receive letters from esteemed friends, and from these also he would read extracts aloud to me.

A short time after the loss of his wife I was able to induce him to renew his automobile rides and his golf and go on an occasional *Mayflower* trip down the Potomac River.

He had keen powers of observation and was especially fond of striking out cross-country for a walk and chatting with farmers or workingmen he met along the road, always anxious to conceal his own identity. On one occasion a farmer said: "You favor the picture of President Wilson." And the President smilingly replied: "Yes, I have often been told that." He greatly preferred that people should not make a to-do over him.

An experience on a *Mayflower* trip illustrates this quality, and at the same time shows him in such a purely human aspect that I am tempted to relate it at length. One afternoon he and I eluded the secret service men by saying that we were going to take a little trip in the motor launch. When we landed at Yorktown we left the sailors in the boat and struck out alone through the streets of the old town, which had practically gone to sleep at three o'clock in the afternoon, and made our way to the Court House. In one of the rooms an old man was sitting at a table writing in a deed book with his coat off, his suspenders much in evidence, and sucking on a corncob pipe. The President asked him if he could see the court-room, and the old gentleman kept writing, and said: "Yep, help yourself. Go right upstairs." The President said: "May I ask who is your Judge?" The reply was: "D. Gardner Tyler, son of the tenth President of the United States, brother of Lyon G. Tyler, President of William and Mary College, which is only twelve miles from here. And our Judge is a fine man too."

All this talking was done without looking up. The fellow never realized the presence of his distinguished visitor. Upon entering the Clerk's Office we met Mr. Hudgins, who very politely acquiesced in the President's request to examine some old documents. Hanging on the wall was a large campaign poster of the President and I was rather surprised that Mr. Hudgins did not seem to recognize the visitor. There he was standing beside a large picture of himself. When we left the Clerk's Office I felt sure that the President had been unrecognized, but later I learned that Mr. Hudgins had realized who his visitor was and had made the statement: "The President did not introduce himself nor his friend and therefore I did not care to push myself forward by introducing myself." The President mightily appreciated this when he heard of it and said: "There was a true gentleman."

If he could have been received in the same way in the public offices in Washington he would have visited them all. But his continual complaint was that the moment he entered a public building all work stopped and everybody flocked about him. During his administration he promised himself that when he was what he called a free man again he was going to visit every public building in the city—a promise which he could not fulfill because of his illness.

We walked around Yorktown, went to the Post Office, bought some postcard pictures of the old Custom House and of Temple Farm, Washington's Headquarters, and of the Nelson House. The Postmaster, who was also the storekeeper, wanted to know if we did not want to buy some "pop" or ginger ale to cool us off on such a hot July day, assuring us that he would "sell it to us right." We did not take advantage of his offer. As we left the store the President noticed a group of citizens tilted back in their chairs against an old spreading tree, some half asleep, some exchanging random remarks, though no one recognized the fact that the President was passing. A group like this always interested him, because he felt that public opinion was made in just such environments; that the people in Washington did not really know public opinion because they did not associate with the vast masses, who, in country stores or outside of them, according to the seasonal conditions, really formed the opinions which settled elections.

As we walked up the street a bright-eyed little girl about twelve years old was the first person in Yorktown to give any evidence that she recognized the presence of the distinguished visitor. She paused and said: "Excuse me, sir, but you certainly do remind me of the pictures of President Wilson." The President smiled. Whereupon she said: "You *are* President Wilson, are you not, sir?"

The President replied: "Yes, I am guilty."

Then she said: "Won't you please wait and let me run and tell my mother. She will be so anxious to see you."

As we were almost at the front door of her mother's house, the mother in a moment was with us and said:

"Won't you come up on the porch in the shade and have a glass of cold tea?"

We accepted the invitation, and while we were drinking our tea she brought out a communion service which proved to be that used in the old Jamestown Church, the first church in Virginia.

Presently the little girl in excitement said: "Look at the crowd coming up the street to see the President." I counted seven people. Among them was the Postmaster who inquired of the President if he might speak to him privately. The President told him to go ahead. He wanted to know if the President would not raise his salary as Postmaster, as he was only getting thirty dollars a month.

The little girl, Elizabeth Shields, to whom the President had taken a great fancy, acted as our guide to the Nelson House, which was next door, but said: "Mr. President, this was Cornwallis' Headquarters. The house you ought to see is the Temple Farm, which was George Washington's Headquarters." The President thanked her and said, "I will."

Accompanied by what the child called "the crowd," we visited the Yorktown Monument, and, leaving there, we got into the launch and proceeded down the river to Temple Farm where we were to see relics of the battlefield. There was no landing at this place and we could only get the boat within ten or fifteen yards of the bank of the river, so we pulled off our shoes, rolled up our trousers, and waded ashore. We scrambled up a steep embankment through the briars and the bees. In the field between us and the house we were attracted by a bull which was taking entirely too much notice of us. He began to paw the earth and bellow, and I, with a sense of responsibility, suggested to the President that we climb the fence and take a roundabout path to the farmhouse. After we got over the fence the President told the story of an Irishman who was chased by a bull and just as he got partly over the fence the bull hit him with his horns and knocked him completely on the other side. Then the bull began to paw and snort and the Irishman remarked: "You may bow and you may scrape as much as you please, but, be golly, if I don't think you meant it."

No man I have ever known was more quietly indifferent to danger than Mr. Wilson. He told me once that until he was over forty years of age he had the uncomfortable feeling that he did not know for a certainty whether or not he would be a coward in peril; but he was on a ship which went up on an iceberg, stove in her bow, and dropped back into the water seriously damaged, that none knew but what she might go down quickly, and that the perfect calmness which he felt on that occasion reassured him that he would never be a coward no matter what the physical peril.

He gave an example of his contempt for danger in 1914 when he led the funeral procession in New York of the Marines who had been killed at Vera Cruz. The secret service force unearthed a plot to assassinate him and begged him to review the parade from a stand.

Mayor Mitchel of New York added his entreaties, saying: "The country cannot afford to have its President killed."

"The country cannot afford to have a coward for President," was Mr. Wilson's brief and conclusive answer.

CHAPTER

6

WE PLAYED GOLF REGULARLY on the different courses in and about Washington, though he preferred the course across the river in Virginia to all others. He liked the game but he played chiefly from a sense of duty. He had taken up the game too late to become an expert player and his eye trouble was an additional interference. Nevertheless, he was a fair player, due chiefly to his great powers of concentration upon the ball. His approach and putting were the best parts of his game. Here accuracy and carefulness counted for most. The President delighted to quote a definition of golf as, "An ineffectual attempt to put an elusive ball into an obscure hole with implements ill-adapted to the purpose."

I told him that as teachers had Saturdays for holidays, he, as a former teacher, ought to take at least a portion of Saturday for golf, and so he formed the habit of having an early breakfast on Saturday morning, followed by a game of golf. At that time I was living in the Avondale Apartment, and I arrived one morning feeling tired and looking the same. He said to me: "Doctor, you look tired. Is everything all right with you?" And I replied that I had been up most of the night with an old lady who was sick in the Avondale. He was quick at catching up people on their forms of speech, and he remarked whimsically: "I know something of human anatomy but would you mind telling me in what part of the body the Avondale is located?"

He was frequently criticized for exclusiveness in the choice of his companions in golf, but the fact of the matter is that he did not want business mingled with his recreation, and he soon found that most men whom he invited to play with him insisted on introducing public business into the conversation.

He did one thing at a time. When he worked, he worked to the exclusion of everything from his mind except the matter in hand, and he carried the same spirit into his diversions.

He was genuinely fond of automobile rides and knew all the courses around Washington, every turning point. He was fond of repeating the same ride often. The chauffeur was continually under his direction, to whom he would give orders to turn to the right or turn to the left or keep straight on, or reduce speed, for he never cared for rapid driving.

He was strictly obedient to the traffic laws and very considerate of all other automobilists. On warm summer evenings he would often fall asleep while motoring, but it was light slumber from which he was easily awakened.

A characteristic incident occurred one evening when a bicycle policeman stopped the car far out on Sixteenth Street. There was a brief colloquy between the policeman and the secret service man on the front seat, but the moment the policeman recognized the car he stepped back in embarrassment. Just then Mr. Wilson awoke and asked: "What is the matter?"

And the secret service man said: "Mr. President, there is such confusion in orders about lights that nobody knows what is the latest order."

Whereupon Mr. Wilson said: "Call the policeman here."

The policeman advanced, saluting shyly and saying: "It's all right, Mr. President. I didn't know it was you."

To which Mr. Wilson answered: "Tell me what is the matter. If we are disobeying any law I must know it. I am not exempt from the law. On the contrary, I of all people must observe the laws."

Though he played golf, rode in his automobile, took trips on the *Mayflower*, I knew that these were only temporary diversions, and that at heart he was desperately lonely.

It may be asked why I did not arrange to fill the house with company. I did what I could but Mr. Wilson had never been a man to find solace in crowds. He preferred to dine with me or with a few other invited friends.

On her return from Cornish, Miss Margaret, now the presiding lady of the White House, did all in her power to alleviate her father's loneliness, as did Miss Bones, his cousin, whom Mrs. Wilson had brought to the White House with her as an affectionate companion. Mr. and Mrs. McAdoo visited the house continually, and Mr. and Mrs. Sayre were there as much as Mr. Sayre's duties as a college professor would permit.

Early in 1915 Mrs. Sayre's first son was born, and the President tenderly took his first grandchild in his arms. His sister, Mrs. Howe, her daughter, Mrs. Cothran, and Mrs. Cothran's fascinating child, Josephine, were with him a great deal. It was for Josephine that he set up a Christmas tree and decorated it with his own hands in 1914. He and his brother Joseph, who was living in Baltimore, exchanged frequent visits; but with all his love for those nearest to him, and with all his loving kindness for friends and relatives, there was a void in his heart. It was the habit of his heart to concentrate, and I saw the summer merge into autumn and autumn succeeded by winter and spring and summer, and knew that however bravely he smiled upon the world he was lonely.

CHAPTER

7

THEN AS BY ACCIDENT—he would have said by Providence—he met one who was destined to fill the vacant space.

When Miss Bones was recuperating from a serious illness a mutual friend introduced her to Mrs. Norman Galt, a member of the distinguished Bolling family of Virginia. Since the death of her husband six years before, she had lived quietly in Washington, well known as one of the most beautiful and gracious women in the city but strikingly indifferent to society in the usual sense of the term. She centered her affection upon the members of her family, her mother and sisters and brothers and a few friends. A reciprocal friendship grew up between her and Miss Bones. She and Mr. Wilson were unacquainted, though he had seen her once when he and I were riding together and I had bowed to her. "Who is that beautiful lady?" the President had asked.

One afternoon he and I, returning from a golf

game, were just getting out of the elevator when we met Miss Bones and Mrs. Galt, who was leaving the White House after a visit to Miss Bones. There was a moment's pause while Mrs. Galt and Mr. Wilson were introduced to each other. A second time when we were returning from golf Miss Bones asked us to come in and have a cup of tea with her and her friend, Mrs. Galt.

Out of such random and casual meetings there grew an acquaintanceship in which destiny seemed to play its part, for by degrees Mr. Wilson fell in love with Mrs. Galt, and she, whose closest friends believed it impossible that she should ever marry again, reciprocated.

She found in Woodrow Wilson a man to admire and then to love. The glamor of the White House meant nothing to her. She was as indifferent as he to the pomp of office, was domestic in all her tastes. They seemed made for each other—two splendid, lofty spirits, indifferent to display and to the clamor of the world.

Yet these two together played for several years the most conspicuous roles in the greatest drama of the World's War. In Europe they mingled with kings and queens, and among all the crowned heads she was the queenliest figure of them all. Like her husband, she could "walk with kings nor lose the common touch."

They were quietly married from her modest home in Twentieth Street on December 18, 1915. To his family and to hers the marriage brought extreme gratification, for all who knew them both knew that an ordeal of loneliness had ended. The Wilson girls saw in Mrs. Edith Wilson the deliverer of their father from sadness into joy, and she, in turn, always showed the utmost consideration and affection for them.

From their wedding day until Mr. Wilson's death, a period of eight years and a month and a half, she was practically always at his side. With dynamic vitality and sheer joy of living she showed him how to take hold again of life and happiness. It would be a great record to recite her participation in his political career and his triumphs at home and abroad (her beautiful face and radiant smile captivated the multitudes), but the acme of her greatness was revealed when he fell ill—her staunchness, her devotion, her cheerfulness under a strain of four and a half years, which would have broken in spirit or health a woman less strong.

For more than a year while he remained in office an invalid she had to stand between him and the public. When he was prostrated and it seemed, as she herself said, cruelty to disturb him with public affairs, it frequently happened that the business was too vital to be kept from his attention. It was then that Mrs. Wilson had to listen to Cabinet officers or delegations from the Hill, take the matter to her husband, and report back his decisions. Physically he was very weak but mentally very alert, with no lessening of his old power to sweep aside accumulations of detail and reach into the core of the matter. At the same time, his sense of humor was ever present.

Some thought it flattery to tell her that she was governing the country and doing it extraordinarily well. "Do you call that a compliment?" was her scornful retort. She said to personal friends that she made it her object to understand clearly the business which was under consideration and to report it in as precise language as possible to her husband. She was a great reporter. She has said that she was trained to accuracy when she was a child because her mother would tell her to be sure to observe closely anything that she saw or heard in the town of Wytheville and repeat it to one of her grandparents who was an invalid.

Mrs. Wilson's firmness was equal to her husband's, and she stood like a stone wall between the sickroom and the officials who insisted that their business was so important that they must see him. "The welfare of the country depends upon our presenting this case to him in person," said one delegation. To which she made the memorable reply: "I am not thinking of the country now, I am thinking of my husband." During the four and a half years of his illness she thought of practically nothing else.

After a while he grew strong enough to see officials when necessary, to sit on the rear balcony of the White House and read state papers or have her read them to him, and to sign public documents. An official remarked that in his department they had a barometer of the President's increasing strength in the increasing firmness of his signature.

As he recuperated Mrs. Wilson drove with him every afternoon, read to him, watched motion pictures with him in the East Room, occasionally conferred at his request with some official, was always at his side or at his call. As she read to him in the mornings on the portico, or in the evenings in the Oval Room, his comments showed how closely he followed. At that time they were reading a good deal of historical fiction, especially Stanley Weyman's, and Mr. Wilson's commentaries, if they had been taken down and incorporated in one of the volumes, would have made a good school textbook.

After he retired to private life in S Street, she was still continually at his side. Her whole day was regulated by his regime. Her brief social engagements and her business errands downtown were set for hours when he would be occupied by his voluminous correspondence, which he dictated to his brother-in-law, Mr. John Randolph Bolling. During the rest of the morning she would read aloud to him, would sit and chat with him while he ate his lunch, and, while he rested after the meal, she would have her own lunch either with her brother or with a few privileged friends. As soon as his nap was finished she would start with him on his afternoon automobile ride, returning from which she sat in the living room talking with him or reading to him, and occasionally receiving a few guests with him. He had his dinner in the living room and she sat frequently reading to him from the day's newspapers or from a book, and after dinner he would go upstairs to his bedroom. She would then have her dinner, and if she had guests they always understood that she would leave them shortly after dinner to go to her husband's room and be with him until he felt inclined to sleep.

She was one of the most practical of women. The things she could accomplish in the little periods at her disposal were astonishing. She kept no house-keeper but directed her own household. She had executive genius and took upon herself the responsi-bilities and burdens of many. She was devoted to her mother and her somewhat frail sister. These two were the most frequent companions of Mr. and Mrs. Wilson on their automobile rides. On one of the after-noons while her husband was slowly dying and she was sitting at his bedside in sorrow she ordered the servant to have the automobile sent to take her mother and sister for a drive in the fresh air. She did not forget that they, too, were sitting in tense anxiety and she wanted them to have such recreation as they might.

Mr. Wilson's health had apparently improved dis-tinctly in the summer of 1923, and I assured her that there was no risk in her going away for a few days' rest, which she so much needed. Since the autumn of 1919 she had not been outside of the city of Washing-ton except for a trip or two to Baltimore. Her husband was my strong supporter in urging her to accept three invitations for brief visits out-of-town, once with Mr. and Mrs. Baruch in New York on the occasion of Lord Robert Cecil's visit to this country, once to Mr. and Mrs. Charles S. Hamlin's country place at Mattapoisett in Massachusetts, and once with Mr. and Mrs. Norman Davis in New York. Occasionally she would accept a luncheon engagement with the understanding that she must be back home at a stated moment to go driving with her husband. Once in a while she would go to the theatre, of which she was very fond, with a few friends, and all the while in anxiety or in periods of relief she turned on the world a smiling face.

A physician gets to know human nature well, both in sick people and in those who are near and dear to them. The strength, the fortitude, the courage, and the constancy of Mrs. Wilson were the greatest I have ever known. The anxiety that was eating at her heart she concealed even from those who were near to her, even when she was at the breaking point. There were times when she would have broken had it not been for her tremendous will power.

CHAPTER

8

THE QUESTION of Mr. Wilson's attending the Peace Conference in person has been debated from many angles. Even after the Armistice he still discussed the feasibility of his sitting in person in the Conference. But the more he conferred, studied reports from abroad, and reflected on the situation, the more convinced he became that the Allies would insist upon a peace of force and vengeance, while he, always looking further ahead than any other man, knew that only on a peace of justice could a stabilized Europe be rebuilt. Also he was convinced that tantamount to a continuing peace there must be a bond of nations, in which each sovereign state should enter into compact with all other states to prevent a recurrence of the wrongs which had begotten the Great War. He believed—and the sequel showed the correctness of his prevision—that there would be an outcry for immediate peace terms and a demand to postpone the formation of an association of nations to some future time,

whereas he knew that the only way to secure a real
and vital compact of nations was to interknit it with
the treaty of peace. Such was his faith, and he was
fully aware that he himself must be the chief apostle
of that faith and the chief champion of that cause in
the face of many who called themselves "realists" and
would demand that the business of the day be dealt
with rather than future contingencies. And so it became to him a matter of conscience to head in person
the American Peace Commission. He *must* go.

Furthermore, because he knew that he would have
to resist strong opposition abroad and then fight a
backfire at home, it became clear to his mind that he
should choose fellow-commissioners who presumably
would work harmoniously with him. There would be
no spare time for dealing with divisions in his own
household while fighting enemies in front and behind.
With that object in view he selected Colonel E.M.
House, who had been his political adviser from the
beginning of his Administration; the Honorable
Robert Lansing, the Secretary of State; General
Tasker H. Bliss, for whom the President had acquired
a high respect; and the Honorable Henry White, a
Republican, who had been Ambassador to Italy and
to France, and in whose unselfish and nonpartisan
patriotism the President had complete faith.

We crossed the ocean four times, for Mr. Wilson
made a brief visit to the United States in February-
March, 1919, to attend to necessary business incident
to the closing of Congress on March 4th. On each of

the voyages he transacted an immense amount of work in an improvised office aboard the *George Washington,* but he also found time for relaxation, for conversations with those who accompanied him, for visits to motion picture plays in the evening, and of course for regular church attendance on Sundays. It was like him to go below one Sunday and worship with the sailors and enlisted men in the "Old Salt Theatre" instead of attending service with the officers and the distinguished coterie of diplomats in the upper quarters. He always did things of this sort simply and without ostentation, sometimes without previous warning. When he appeared unannounced in the "Old Salt Theatre," there was much scurrying about to find seats for him and Mrs. Wilson and myself.

On the first journey across there were three trusted newspapermen with whom Mr. Wilson had several frank talks in which he outlined the purpose of the mission. These three were: R.J. Bender of the United Press; J.E. Nevin of the International News Service, and L.C. Probert of the Associated Press. In one of these talks he said:

The plot is thickening! I think it now is necessary that we get a clear comprehension of exactly my position in this situation. As you know, Clemenceau, Lloyd George, and Orlando have held a meeting in London. Colonel House was unable to be there. He has not yet been able to throw off his attack of influenza as rapidly as he expected. The men apparently got together on a programme which I have

just received. It was badly garbled in cable; hence the
delay in my getting it. It is very obvious in reading
between the lines of Colonel House's report to me
that these representatives of France, Great Britain,
and Italy are determined to get everything out of
Germany that they can. They know Germany is down
and out. Instead of going about the thing in the fair
way, namely, determine what they think they are
justly entitled to demand of Germany and then seek
the means of securing it through learning how Germany may be expected to meet the demands—if she
can meet them at all—and arranging their claims
accordingly, they favor the appointment of a commission to study exactly what Germany has got today
and the naming of another commission to apportion
what Germany has among the governments that have
fought her in this war. I am absolutely opposed to
this. A statement that I once made that this should
be a "peace without victory" holds more strongly
today than ever. The peace that we make must be
one in which justice alone is the determining factor.

Upon the first occasion that I have after meeting
these gentlemen and letting them know what sort of
a fellow I am and giving myself the opportunity of
determining what sort of chaps they are, I will say
to them, if necessary, that we are gathered together,
not as the masters of anyone, but that we are the
representatives of a new world met together to determine the greatest peace of all times. It must not be
a peace of loot or spoliation. If it were such we would
be an historical scourge. I for one shall, if necessary,
tell them that if that is the kind of peace they demand, I will withdraw personally and with my
commissioners return home and in due course take
up the details of a separate peace. Of course, I do not

believe that that will come to pass. I think once we
get together they will know that we stand for no
bargaining but will hold firmly by the principles we
have set forth; and once they learn that that is my
purpose, I think we can come to an agreement
promptly.

He struck the keynote there of his attitude throughout the entire conference. When matters reached an
impasse in the following spring and he cabled orders
for the *George Washington* to be taken out of dry-
dock in the Brooklyn Navy Yard and sent to Brest,
there was consternation. Some thought it was a mere
threat. Even one of the American Commission hinted
to M. Clemenceau that "orders are not always
executed." The French Premier asked me my opinion,
and I told him that President Wilson never made
empty threats, adding: "If he ever starts for Brest to
go aboard the *George Washington,* you and your
entire French army cannot turn him back."

CHAPTER

9

Hɪs ʀᴇᴄᴇᴘᴛɪᴏɴ in Europe was without parallel in history. In Paris the throngs along the sidewalks cheered and wept, hailing him as the savior of France. Though he arrived in London on Boxing Day, when the streets are generally deserted, there were greater crowds in the streets, it was said, than had ever collected before, calling out in chorus, "We want Wilson."

With the solemn and set purpose of his journey there mingled many little incidents which are vivid in my memory. The President and the King took to each other like old friends, and, indeed, the King was a man whom anybody could approach with easy manner and jests. For instance, he asked me if everything was being provided for my comfort, and I told him: "The servant who has been detailed to look after my comfort is not only very attentive but accompanies me whenever I walk around the Palace; in fact, he is so attentive that I am beginning to wonder if he is not watching me."

An incident occurred between this same servant and myself to which the President frequently referred with laughter. I had been exposed for a considerable part of the day to British cold and dampness, and Buckingham Palace was not as warmly heated as most of our American houses, so that when I got to my quarters in the Palace I was chilled all through. Presently my attendant appeared, tall as a Grenadier, dressed in a white wig, red coat, black velvet knee-trousers, white silk stockings, and large silver buckles on his shoes. Bowing gracefully, he asked me, in pronounced cockney: "Will you have your tea now, sir?" It was hard to get through his head that any man would not take afternoon tea, but when I finally made it clear to him that I really did not want any tea at all, he asked: "Is there anything else I can bring you?" Now, I was under the impression that Buckingham Palace was dry during the war, but I was very cold and I knew exactly what my case called for, so I said: "I am feeling chilly, I have a sore throat, and my shoulders are aching, and I think I am catching cold." In other words, I made all the excuses a Virginian makes to get a drink, but the difficulty of the situation was that I was talking Virginian and he was talking British cockney and neither of us understood each other very well. At last I thought I would have to use the actual word which expressed my desires, but I spoke it in too low a voice for him to catch it. I said, "whiskey." He was embarrassed and asked me:

"Will you please repeat your order, sir?" This time I did so by asking him if I could have some Haig & Haig. He bowed, as one who understands, and left the room. After an interval he returned with two soft-boiled eggs on a platter. Whereupon, I felt that it was only proper courtesy in Buckingham Palace to eat one of those eggs, thinking all the while what my Culpeper friends would think of my acceptance of such a substitute.

The King and the President enjoyed exchanging jokes, and each seemed to understand the other's brand of humor. The King told the President how he had once been reviewing some American troops during the war when he overheard one of our doughboys ask (pointing to the King): "Who is that bug over there?" To which his buddy replied: "Shut up, you fool, don't you know that's the King?" Then the first doughboy replied: "King hell. If he's the King where is his crown?"

The King laughingly told the President that as far as he was concerned he did not mind being called a bug but the idea that he would go to inspect he-men wearing a crown was ridiculous.

At Buckingham Palace there was a joke on the President which had wide currency. He and Mrs. Wilson were being photographed with the King and Queen and Princess Mary, and when the picture was developed it was observed that Mr. Wilson had by accident one trouser leg turned up. There was much comment on this incident, but the British people seemed to take it as typical of an American President not to care anything about precise formalities.

At Manchester we had many amusing experiences at the Town Hall and as guests of the Lord Mayor and Lady Mayoress, but I shall repeat only one characteristic act of the President. When he arose to speak to a great audience they also arose, as we learned subsequently from the Lord Mayor, without any pre-arrangement, and sang spontaneously from beginning to end, "For He's a Jolly Good Fellow." And when they had finished the President opened his remarks by telling them the story of Oliver Herford, who was sitting in a restaurant when a stranger clapped him on the shoulder and said, "Hello, Ollie," and he looked up and said: "I don't know your name and I don't recognize your face, but your manners are very familiar." And from that the President went on to say that though Manchester was a complete stranger to him, he found its manners delightfully familiar.

It would be impossible to say where the President received the most magnificent ovation. Certainly nothing could surpass that of London, but all of us who saw the reception in Rome carry an unforgettable memory of the spontaneous crowds and enthusiasm in the ancient city. King Victor Emmanuel and the President seemed to get on extremely well together, though there was almost an embarrassing small incident when the King and Queen were the official guests of Mr. and Mrs. Wilson at the American Embassy. Ambassador Thomas Nelson Page had coached Mr. Wilson and told him that when the asparagus was served it would be the signal for the President to arise and toast the King. But, unfortunately, the Ambassador forgot to tell Mrs. Page this, and she, therefore, had no asparagus on the menu. The President, watching in vain for a signal that was never given, had to take matter in his own hand, and, before dessert was brought on, arose and made a graceful speech in honor of His Majesty.

At Milan in the great Cathedral Square the crowds were massive, and there was a reverence everywhere that touched the President deeply. Candles were burned before his picture, his signature was kissed and pressed to men's hearts. Seeing this the President, by nature a philosopher, grew very solemn. He said: "There is bound to be a reaction to this sort of thing. I am now at the apex of my glory in the hearts of these people, but they are thinking of me only as one who has come to save Italy, and I have got to pool the interests of Italy with the interests of all the world, and when I do that I am afraid they are going to be disappointed and turn about and hiss me."

This was prophetic. It was not long before the reaction which he had foreseen set in. And it manifested itself first in Italy, because Italy desired possession of Fiume and full control of the Adriatic Sea. Such demands were incompatible with President Wilson's conception of full justice to small nations and a seaport for Jugoslavia. The relapse in Italy and elsewhere was not Woodrow Wilson's failure, but the failure of nations and their leaders to look as far ahead as he, to comprehend the real meaning of his mission and his doctrine. While he was pleading for world harmony, others were too often thinking of national ambition.

But at the time of his arrival in Europe the populace had recognized in him the champion of the people. They were war-worn, and weary of the old processes which, since the beginning of historic time, had led to conflict, slaughter, plunder, devastation, and misery. They were tired of the old diplomacies which always culminated in war. They saw in Mr. Wilson a deliverer from the old order and the originator of a new and better plan. His words had reached vaster multitudes in all parts of the world than the words of any other man. They were straightforward words, and, therefore, understandable by plain people—words which voiced the aspiration of the multitude. His personal magnetism seemed to overcome the handicap of foreign language as far as his Continental hearers were concerned. In Paris, at the Sorbonne, or in the Italian Chamber, the President spoke in English, as he did everywhere, and there could have been only a small percentage who understood. President Wilson spoke no foreign language. "To know English properly," he said, "has kept me so busy all my life that I haven't had time for anything else." But they seemed to understand him. It was a very striking tribute to the power of his personality.

It was humanly impossible to prevent the reaction which followed within a year. Astute politicians distorted his language and interpreted to the people a meaning different, often diametrically opposed, to what it really meant. This was going on in America, in France, in Italy. The poison worked into the minds of the people, and for a while it seemed as if Mr. Wilson would never live to see himself vindicated. But he did. Long before he died, while politicians were reviling him, and weak-kneed supporters were apologizing for his mistakes, there was a popular swing back to him. Plain people everywhere, those who had no interest in the political game, saw that this man had caught a vision of a future of peace and happiness and had plainly pointed the way to it. They saw that the world in rejecting him had rejected its own restoration to order and stabilized peace.

CHAPTER

10

H<small>E WAS A STATESMAN</small>, a war President, a leader in international councils, but he was always a teacher. A great teacher is an interpreter and Woodrow Wilson was the interpreter of the deepest lying political aspirations of collective peoples, a desire to be unmolested by the wiles of scheming diplomats and the ravages of conquest.

Now death has set its sacred seal upon his mission, and we know beyond question that his principles were right. In the present confusion of the world there is scarcely a straight-thinking man who does not realize that by the spirit which Woodrow Wilson sought to introduce into the world, the world must be saved. Many still discountenance his methods, but all know that his ideas and ideals must galvanize whatever methods shall be devised for peace and reconstruction.

As from the tomb at Mount Vernon people get fresh impulse for their faith in individual liberty, so from the tomb in the Cathedral of Mount Saint Alban people will always gather new inspiration from Woodrow Wilson's controlling idea of the equality of nations, small and great, and of international peace founded, not on strength of arms, but on justice. "Justice" was to him no empty word, as "liberty" was to Washington no empty word. Mr. Wilson knew that complete world justice could not be won by a word, or a single act, but he believed with all his mighty intellect and all his fighting soul that the hour had come to make a beginning and to make it with as little compromise as possible.

Between him and many with whom he conferred, there was a conflict between the ideas of a peace of justice and a peace of vengeance. Most of the French officials were unable to understand Mr. Wilson's calmness. They did not realize that he as much as any of them hated Germany and all her ways but that he was holding himself in hand because he knew that peace terms drawn up in furious rage would defeat their own ends, that to destroy Germany economically would make just reparations impossible. Besides, he continued to hold to his distinction between the German war authorities and the German people. The German people had done evil, but it was done under wrong leadership. He felt that to keep cool was the first essential to the making of a peace of justice.

French officials continually urged him to visit the devastated regions, and he kept postponing, saying to his friends: "They want me to see red, and I can't afford to see red. To whip myself into a passion of rage would be to unfit myself for the present task. I know well enough the wrong that Germany has done, and Germany must be punished, but in justice, not in frenzy."

We had made brief trips to the American Head-quarters at Chaumont and to Château-Thierry and Rheims, but the French wanted the President to make a much more extensive tour of the ruined area. It was not until Sunday morning, March 23rd, that we took a somewhat extensive tour to the scenes of battle, re-visiting Château-Thierry and Rheims, and visiting for the first time Soissons, the Chemin des Dames, Coucy-le-Château, Chauny, Noyon, Montdidier, and the neighboring regions. The party consisted of the President, Mrs. Wilson, Miss Benham (Mrs. Wilson's secretary), and myself. We were followed by the necessary secret service guard but were not accompanied by any military aides.

The President was intensely interested in each spot that we visited and the informality of our visit enabled me to get some of the human reactions toward him from the French people, both military and civilian.

Coucy contained a famous old château, which was destroyed by the Germans in their retreat in 1916. When the President looked at the ruins, he shook his head and said: "What a pity that a place like this should be destroyed when there was no military or other advantage to be gained—only wantonness."

Leaving Coucy we journeyed to various places, including Noyon, Lassigny, and Montdidier. All along this section the American troops had taken the most heroic part.

At the little town of St. Maxence the President's car stopped to take oil and gas and was surrounded by French people, old men and old women, as well as French soldiers and many little children. They acclaimed the President as the savior of the world and appealed to him to stand by the common people of France to bring about a peace which would be a peace for the people. This same sentiment had been expressed by a French officer at Soissons, who told me that the soldiers wanted the President to know that they were back of him in his plans for peace and did not want him to allow France to get the kind of peace that Clemenceau and the French commission were desirous of having made. They declared that a Clemenceau peace would favor the capitalists, but that they had such faith in the President of the United States that they knew he would give them a peace that would be just to all.

On his return to Paris the President said:

> The day has been very instructive to me. It has been in many ways exceedingly painful, because what I saw was deeply distressing, but it has enabled me to have a fuller conception than ever of the extraordinary sufferings and hardships of the people of France in the baptism of cruel fire through which they have passed.

The President's last visit to the stricken areas was to Belgium, a long-contemplated journey which had to be frequently postponed because of the duties which confined him to Paris.

We entrained from Paris on the night of June 17th and the next morning were met by the King and Queen of the Belgians, who had flown by aeroplane from Brussels to meet the Presidential party. The journey through Belgium, which had originally been intended to occupy three days, had to be crowded into two to enable the President to be back in Paris for the concluding business and ceremonies of the Peace Conference. But the King of the Belgians, true to his reputation as a speedy traveller, set a pace in the front car with the President which covered in two days what had been planned for three. I was in the third car and got full benefit of the dust of the preceding cars, averaging fifty miles an hour—the second car being occupied by the Queen of the Belgians and Mrs. Wilson. Miss Margaret Wilson was one of the party, as were also Mr. Herbert Hoover, Mr. Bernard Baruch, Mr. Vance McCormick, and Mr. Norman Davis. Brand Whitlock, United States Minister to Belgium, joined us after we had crossed the frontier.

Among other places we saw the Ypres Canal by which the Belgians flooded the lowlands when the Germans made an effort to break through to the sea; Dixmude and Houthulst Forest, the wooded ranges where the Belgians finally turned back the German assault; Ypres, where the Canadian troops were practically annihilated and where the Germans first used poison gas—all of it wasteland which had been fought over repeatedly, a morass of mud, with half-picked skeletons of horses, wrecked trucks and ambulances, and little clusters of graves marked with crosses. From Ypres we motored through Menin, Roulers, Thourout, and on to Ostende, where we were given a reception by the Burgomaster and practically the entire population of the city.

From Zeebrugge we were driven to a train which bore us to Brussels and were escorted to the palace, one of the most magnificent in Europe, and given a truly royal reception. It was after the party had broken up for the night that I observed great crowds in front of the palace eager for a glimpse of the President. Going to his bedroom I informed him of the situation. Though he was partially undressed, he put on his clothes, went out on a little balcony, and made a brief speech, in the course of which he said: "In coming personally I have merely followed my own heart and the heart of the people of America to Belgium."

The next day our party motored to the Town Hall at Louvain where the President was received by the Burgomaster. In the manuscript room of the ruined university a degree was conferred upon him by Cardinal Mercier. In response the President paid a noble tribute to education and condemned in scathing terms the ruthlessness of the Germans which had led them to this wanton act of destruction, saying that the Germans had misused their own education, that education could be prostituted, and had been when the Germans made their assault upon the ancient University of Louvain.

But this evidence of German atrocity did not swerve the President from his view that the peace terms, however stern, must be made on a basis of justice rather than on a basis of vengeance. He held firmly to the idea that revenge would be only temporary and would sooner or later lead to reprisals and other wars, and that uncompromising justice would lay the foundations for a permanent peace. His idea of justice involved the idea of holding Germany to strict accountability for what she had done, to punish her but not to destroy her economically and nationally.

This fundamental idea of the sort of peace that would be lasting and constructive for the future sometimes brought him into sharp conflict with his conferees, Mr. Lloyd George, M. Clemenceau, and Signor Orlando—able statesmen but none of them possessing the prophetic qualities of Mr. Wilson who looked beyond the immediate results of the Peace Conference to the far-off future of Europe and the world.

I myself was a witness of a scene in the conference room which was as dramatic as anything ever played upon a stage. In the intensity of the debates feeling sometimes ran high and men would say things on the impulse of the moment which they would not have uttered in calmer circumstances.

One morning the three Premiers grew so passionate in their opposition to Mr. Wilson's calmer, forward-

looking policy that they accused him of being pro-
German. I happened to enter the room just as they
were about to recess for lunch. Mr. Wilson told me a
little of what had occurred, but for the most part was
quite silent at the lunch table. After lunch he asked
me to ride with him in the Bois. He was very silent
but I could see that he was thinking deeply and that
his emotions were profoundly stirred. When we returned to the house and just before we got out of the
motor he said to me: "I want you to come into the
room with me. Those men this morning accused me
of being pro-German. They have gone a step too far
and I don't know what may happen." With that he
walked down the hallway, very straight, his jaw set,
his eyes fixed. I could see that his fighting blood was
circulating, and there was electricity in the air. In a
moment or two the others came in and all were
seated, and for a few seconds there was intense silence.
Contrary to his usual custom in the Council of Four
he rose from his chair and began to speak standing.
I wish I had a stenographic report of what he said, for
it was certainly one of the greatest speeches of his
whole career. In substance it was to the effect that he
had never liked Germany, that he had never been in
Germany, that he had never cared for the German
methods of education, that no man in the room was
less German-minded than he, and that he resented
deeply the accusations which they had brought against
him at the morning session. Turning to M. Clemenceau, with his eyes ablaze, he said: "And yet you this

morning told me that I should be wearing the Kaiser's helmet. And why? Because I have protested against laying a taxation upon Germany which will make life so unattractive to the little children and the children yet unborn that existence would be a running sore and dreams of vengeance an obsession. I am not thinking only of Germany. I am thinking about the future of the world. I am thinking of the inevitable results of a so-called peace founded merely upon revenge. Such ideas belong to the old order. We are facing a new world with new conditions. We are trying to stabilize a world that has been thrown into chaos. One reason why France has had the sympathy of most of the world in this terrible war is because individuals and nations have remembered with indignation the terms which Germany imposed upon France after the Franco-Prussian War—the insolence and the inhumanity of it all. This is why most of the nations have become allies of France—because she had been wronged. I want to save France from being put in the place of Germany in the future. If we do wrong around this peace table the sympathy of the world will some day turn to Germany as it has turned to France in this war. I want to save the whole world from repetitions of such disasters as the world has experienced during the last four years. I know that you men are going the wrong way about it, and I know that I am right, because I know human nature and the processes of war. I am for a severe punishment for Germany but a just one."

While he was speaking M. Clemenceau made a motion to rise from his chair. Mr. Wilson whirled around upon him and said: "You sit down. I did not interrupt you when you were speaking this morning." M. Clemenceau sank back in his chair.

Then Mr. Wilson continued—and I am giving only an inadequate idea of what he said and how he said it—that he was speaking as an advocate of the little children, that he wanted them to be saved from what their fathers and their elder brothers had been through, that he wanted to stem and stop the floods of blood with which Europe had been drenched, that the supreme purpose of this war had been to make it a means of ending war. He said: "Therefore I cannot consent to be a party to the kind of adjustment that you men counsel because it is no adjustment. It is merely laying fire for the future. It is not only the innocent children of Germany that I am thinking of. I am thinking of the children of France, of England, of Italy, of Belgium, of my own United States, of the whole world. I see their little faces turn toward us in unconscious pleading that we shall save them from annihilation. I am not asking for a soft peace but for a righteous peace."

Again M. Clemenceau rose from his chair and slowly approached Mr. Wilson, this time with moisture in his eyes. Taking the President's hand in both of his, he said: "Mr. President, I want to say that you are not only a great man but you are a good one, and I am with you." There was tense silence. In his chair

Mr. Lloyd George sat, nodding approval, and Signor Orlando was standing over by the window softly sobbing.

He had many a tilt with Mr. Lloyd George, M. Clemenceau, and Signor Orlando, but his personal relationships with them were generally pleasant and cordial. He had been accused in America of inability to work with other people. This was never so—at home or abroad. His daily conferences with the three Premiers were patient and oftentimes humorous. Both he and M. Clemenceau had quick powers of repartee. On another occasion when the French Premier was arguing for reparations and taxation which, in the President's judgment, would crush Germany economically, M. Clemenceau, in retort to the President's objections, exclaimed: "You have a heart of steel," to which the President promptly replied: "But I have not the heart to steal."

CHAPTER

11

I DO NOT PROPOSE to write a detailed or technical account of Mr. Wilson's health history, but I am aware that in these recollections of him, the public will expect from his physician something more than the random references to his health which have already occurred in this volume.

Constitutionally, he had not been strong either as a youth, a young man, or a man in early middle age. An attack of measles had gone hard with him at Davidson College, preventing him from completing his freshman year there, forcing him to return to his father's home in Wilmington, North Carolina, where he spent a year in recuperation and in preparation to enter Princeton. The aftereffects of this malady prevented him, to his extreme regret, from taking violent exercise, though he was so deeply interested in college athletics that he became the manager of the baseball team. Again, poor health prevented him from graduating in law from the University of Virginia. At Bryn

Mawr and Wesleyan he had to take good care of himself in order to discharge his professorial duties. As Professor and President of Princeton he was frequently under the care of physicians for a stubborn stomach ailment, and three times he broke down. In the first attack he suffered from neuritis, of which he was not entirely cured until he became President of the United States. In the second attack he was operated upon for hemorrhoids and developed phlebitis. In the third and most serious attack there was a retinal hemorrhage in his left eye, which partially destroyed the sight of that organ. In spite of all this, his iron will and perfect equanimity enabled him to do an increasing amount of work each year, but he had not cultivated habits of regular exercise and periodical recreation.

When he entered the White House and I became acquainted with the physical man I was confident that if I could get his coöperation in carrying out daily the simple laws of health, he would, barring accident, carry through to the end, though one of the most eminent physicians of the country, Dr. Weir Mitchell, prophesied that the new President could not possibly outlive his first term. Careful examination and all the medical tests revealed that there was no organic disease, but much sedentary life had been bad for a constitution not naturally vigorous, and he was below par. It was a clear case for preventive medicine.

With his confidence and coöperation, four outstanding elements of treatment and of his own personality kept him going under conditions that would soon have exhausted the powers of a younger and stronger man. These four things were system, exercise, a sense of humor, and food suited to his idiosyncrasies. The last I was able to ascertain after some experimentation. He was the most obedient patient a physician ever had. He grew steadily stronger. He worked as few Presidents have worked and bore burdens such as few men have been called upon to shoulder. The remarkable thing is not that he broke down finally, but that, with his constitution and his burdens, he kept well by obedience to the simple laws of health. At the conclusion of the Armistice he was stronger than he had ever been in his life, notwithstanding all he had gone through.

Nevertheless I dreaded the added strain of his personal attendance upon the Peace Conference. I foresaw that he would be in almost daily contest with antagonists. I knew that he would see sights which would drain his emotions, and I feared that in a new environment it would be impossible for him to maintain the systematic habits of life which had sustained him at home even during the struggle of war. There was something else which I did not foresee, an attack of influenza in Paris, which proved to be one of the contributory causes of his final breakdown. But I could not argue with his conscience. All I could do was to accompany him and take the best medical care of him possible.

When he took his seat at the Peace table he was

sixty-two years old. Had he considered his health, had he put prudence and caution first, he would not have embarked for Europe on December 4, 1918. Then and there he deliberately neglected his health. Then and there for the first time he deliberately refused to obey his physician and the laws of health which he so well understood. Duty was for him superior to his health.

My worst fears were realized. There was the hurry and flurry of official engagements. He met most of the important people in Europe. He addressed crowds such as no man had ever faced before in Great Britain, France, Italy, and Belgium. He was in continual struggle with the representatives of the allied and associated nations, he standing single and alone among them for a principle which seemed to them too far off to grasp. He was forced to break in upon his regular regimen, to forego exercise, to work at all hours day and night and even on Sundays. His emotions were torn by sights of pain and sorrow everywhere, in the devastated regions and in the hospitals.

His tender heart bled for each afflicted soldier in the hospital wards. Soon after his arrival in France he and Mrs. Wilson visited the hospital at Neuilly. For most of the soldiers the President had a word of good fellowship, but it was noticed that in shaking hands with one soldier he said nothing. This soldier, who had been blinded, asked the nurse why the President had held his hand so long, gripped it so hard, and said nothing. We who were with him and watching him knew, for we had seen his face working for self-control, a film cover his eyes, a clutch in his throat. We observed the same significant silence in another ward when the President asked a splendid specimen of manhood on crutches and at attention how it was that so many of the men were bereft of a leg. The soldier answered: "Those who were shot higher up are not here, sir." The President's lip quivered as he passed silently down the line.

That afternoon he and Mrs. Wilson visited all the wards of one of the French hospitals. In one ward a blinded French soldier stood erect and sang "The Marseillaise." To the end of his life, the President referred, always with emotion, to that.

At the American cemetery at Suresnes, on a hillside looking toward Paris, the President on Memorial Day, 1919, delivered one of his great addresses, a memorial to the dead, an admonition to the living to be faithful to those things for which their comrades had died. After the ceremonies he went down among the lines of graves, each marked with its cross, and deposited a wreath in behalf of the Boy Scouts of America. As he rose to his feet a French lady approached him and said: "Mr. President, may I be permitted to add these flowers to those which you have just deposited here as a tribute to the American dead, who, in sacrificing their lives, saved the lives of thousands of Frenchmen? My two boys were killed in battle." And then she broke down and cried.

Such incidents, and there were hundreds of them, took their toll from a man who was always under pressure and who beneath a reserved exterior carried the heart of a child, tender, susceptible to the griefs and burdens of others.

I used to beg him to slacken a little the pressure under which he worked, but he would answer: "Give me time. We are running a race with Bolshevism and the world is on fire. Let us wind up this work here and then we will go home and find time for a little rest and play and take up our health routine again."

In the early spring of 1919 came that ill-omened attack of influenza, the insidious effects of which he was not in good condition to resist. Then followed asthma, which broke the sleep that had always been his sheet anchor. In the pressure of public business or private grief he had always been able to sleep, but now asthmatic coughing woke him at intervals all through the night. He was less obedient than he had been to his physician's advice. He insisted on holding conferences while he was still confined to his sickbed. When he was able to get up he began to drive himself as hard as before—morning, afternoon, and frequently evening conferences. Added to all this was to be the final strain at home, a bitter struggle with the United States Senate, and then a tour of the country, for which he was quite unfit physically, and which was the final cause of his collapse. This instead of the "rest and play" to which he had looked forward for many months.

CHAPTER

12

THOUGH BELOW PAR in the spring he worked with all his strength. The conference, which had lasted seven months instead of the few weeks which he had originally thought would be necessary, closed on June 28, 1919, in the Hall of Mirrors in the Palace of Versailles, where old William I of Prussia had been crowned Emperor of Germany nearly fifty years before. The Germans were reaping a sour harvest from the seeds they had shown in the Franco-Prussian War.

In place of the imperial splendor of the earlier scene, as shown in the historical painting of it, the ceremony on June 28th was without spectacular features. In the presence of an immense audience (the French Government had issued twice as many tickets as there was seating capacity) the meeting was opened with a brief address by M. Clemenceau. President Wilson had suggested that the German delegates sign first because if left to sign last they might change their minds, refuse to sign, and make the whole procedure ridiculous. Then the representatives of the allied and associated powers signed in the French alphabetical order of the nations which they represented. This placed the United States (*Etats Unis*) at the head of the list, and, of course, President Wilson was the first of the American delegation to set his signature to the epochal document. He used a pen which he had purchased for Mrs. Wilson several years before and with which he had signed a majority of state papers.

At the conclusion of the ceremonies President Wilson and Premiers Clemenceau and Lloyd George walked into the square in front of the Palace, and the throngs crying "Vive Wilson!" pressed so closely about him that, notwithstanding the troops, the President's own guard had to close around him to protect him from the enthusiasm of the multitude, many wishing to shake his hand, all wishing to see him.

There was to be a brief meeting in the old Senate Chamber to consider questions that were to be decided later, after the President had left. This included the Italian settlement. Baron Sonnino of Italy and Baron Makino of Japan were present at the discussion. In order to get to the Senate Chamber, Clemenceau suggested that the President, Lloyd George, he, and I get in his car. The chauffeur was evidently excited. At any rate, the car ran away and broke through a lattice fence.

After the discussion in the Senate Chamber we had tea, and then the President and I proceeded in his car back to the temporary White House through throngs that lined the streets of Versailles, St. Cloud, and Paris itself—all continuing to cry "Vive Wilson."

Plans had been completed to leave Paris that night (Saturday), and to sail from Brest the next day. On the previous Thursday the President and I were riding past the Longchamp race track, and I said to him: "Don't you think you are too good a Presbyterian to start on a voyage by sailing from Brest on a Sunday? Don't you think you ought to wait and begin the trip on Monday?" The President smiled at me quizzically and said: "Don't you mean that the Grand Prix is to be run on Sunday and that you want to see it? I am not as green as I look." I was too naïve for a master reader of human motives.

At the railway station, Saturday evening, there collected to bid adieu to the President and Mrs. Wilson officials of the various governments, General Pershing and the members of the American Mission, and, in addition to notables galore, there was a dense throng of Parisians, who had come to give President Wilson a final cheer.

President Poincaré of the French Republic and M. Clemenceau were both there. The relationship between President Wilson and President Poincaré had been rather cool, for M. Poincaré was the leader of the peace-for-vengeance group and never caught the Wilsonian vision. But he was punctilious in ceremonial courtesy. Reluctantly, the President had accepted an invitation to a state dinner at the Elysée Palace on

Thursday night at which M. Poincaré toasted him, and the President and Mrs. Wilson the next day paid their formal final call on M. and Mme. Poincaré. And the President and Mme. Poincaré were at the station to do the honors of the Republic in bidding adieu to Mr. and Mrs. Wilson.

M. Clemenceau's attitude was much more personal. I had come to know him well in Paris and learned to enjoy his friendship and satiric humor, under which I saw more sentiment than he usually cared to display to the world, and with it a sincere admiration for President Wilson. As I bade him farewell, he showed deep feeling, remarking: "In saying good-bye to the President I feel that I am saying good-bye to my best friend."

Mr. Lloyd George was not at the station because of the exhaustion due to a recent illness and the strain of the day, but he called at the house before our departure to say good-bye, stayed for half an hour, and concluded his visit with these words to the President: "You have done more than any one man to bring about further cordial relations between England and the United States. You have brought the two countries closer together than any other individual in history."

Before leaving Paris, Clemenceau and Lloyd George had been urging the President to return to Europe after a while, to which the President replied: "That is practically out of the question. Lincoln one time told the story about a little girl who had some blocks with letters on them. She was learning her ABC's with the use of those blocks, and one night before going to bed she was playing with them. When she got into bed she started to say her prayers, but she was so sleepy that all she could say was—'Oh, Lord, I am too sleepy to say my prayers. Here are the blocks and the letters, you spell it out!' " The President applied the story by saying: "I have worked over here and laid down all the principles, rules, and regulations that I could think of. Someone else now will have to take the blocks and spell it out."

When we reached Brest the next day, we boarded the U.S.S. *George Washington,* which had aboard a great number of troops because of the President's insistence that all transport facilities be used for returning soldiers home.

Just before leaving France the President issued this statement:

As I look back over the eventful months I have spent in France, my memory is not of conferences and hard work only, but also of innumerable acts of generosity and friendship which have made me feel how genuine the sentiments of France are towards the people of America and how fortunate I have been to be the representative of our people in the midst of a nation which knows how to show its kindness with so much charm and such open manifestations of what is in its heart. Deeply happy as I am at the prospect of joining my own countrymen again, I leave France with genuine regret, my deep sympathy for her people and belief in her future confirmed, my thought enlarged by the privilege of association with her public men, conscious of more than one affectionate friendship formed, and profoundly grateful for unstinted hospitality and for countless kindnesses which have made me feel welcome and at home. I take the liberty of bidding France God-speed as well as good-bye, and of expressing once more my abiding interest and entire confidence in her future.

CHAPTER

13

We HAD A PLEASANT, uneventful voyage home. The President had to do much work aboard the ship, but he had more time for exercise in walking the decks and for watching motion pictures in the evening. I was pleased by the improvement that I saw in him and got his consent to prolong the journey two days. He was an excellent sailor, always enjoyed the salt air, and never rested anywhere better than at sea.

We arrived in New York Bay July 8th on a sunny afternoon and were met by a squadron of the Atlantic Fleet, and, later, by a huge nondescript flotilla of hundreds of vessels, some bearing the city officials and committees of reception and others loaded to the water line with volunteer welcomers.

After landing in Hoboken we crossed the river by ferry and drove directly to Carnegie Hall, through a city colorful with flags and confetti, and through the greatest crowds that up to that time had ever greeted an individual in the history of America.

The President's address in Carnegie Hall was his first gun in the battle for the ratification of the Treaty. The next was in the United States Senate, where he presented the documents to the body whose ratification was necessary to make our country a participator in the Treaty and Covenant.

As he was ushered into the Senate Chamber he looked completely well again. His step was elastic, his color good, his eyes bright, his figure erect. His attitude was that of a man who had called his associates in government to reason with them but if they would not reason was ready to fight them to the end. His exposition of the meaning of the Covenant was lucid and noble:

> The united power of free nations must put a stop to aggression and the world must be given peace. . . . Shall we or any other free people hesitate to accept this great duty? Dare we reject it and break the heart of the world? . . . The stage is set, the destiny disclosed. It has come about by no plan of our conceiving, but by the hand of God who led us into this way. We cannot turn back. We can only go forward, with lifted eyes and freshened spirit, to follow the vision. It was of this that we dreamed at our birth. America shall in truth show the way. The light streams upon the path ahead, and nowhere else.

These were some of the key sentences of this great address. They remind us again of the faith that was in Woodrow Wilson, the faith that God had selected this epoch for the liberation of mankind from the tyranny of old usages and those outworn methods of international dealing by which misery is sown in the wind and reaped in the whirlwind.

But America was not allowed to "show the way."

This is a personal sketch of Mr. Wilson—not a challenge to controversy. I shall not inquire into or speculate on the motives which prompted some Senators to obstruct his plans; nor shall I comment on the post-war psychology by which the majority of the people, who, on Mr. Wilson's return from Europe undoubtedly favored ratification, became in a few months violently opposed to ratification.

There were conferences between the President and individual Senators, and a notable conference lasting several hours in the East Room between him and the Committee on Foreign Affairs of the Senate. Gradually, however, a spirit of opposition in the Senate increased in strength, and there was a demand for reservations to which the President would not concede because he believed such reservations would emasculate the Covenant.

His faith in the people was complete, and he felt that if he could get before them the truth about the Treaty and the Covenant they would rally to his banner. I dreaded the extensive journey necessary for this more than I dreaded the plague. I had already seen that the wear and tear on him of continual controversy over the treaty was undoing the good that had been done by his ocean voyage, and that his vitality was being slowly sapped.

I succeeded in persuading him to cancel plans

formed for the journey in early August, but, later on, the conviction grew upon him that he must go. Opposition to the Treaty was increasing in the Senate, and he must rally the moral opinion of the country and do it immediately, so he felt. I played my last card and lost. Going into the study one morning I found the President seated at his desk writing. He looked up and said: "I know what you have come for. I do not want to do anything foolhardy but the League of Nations is now in its crisis, and if it fails I hate to think what will happen to the world. You must remember that I, as Commander in Chief, was responsible for sending our soldiers to Europe. In the crucial test in the trenches they did not turn back—and I cannot turn back now. I cannot put my personal safety, my health in the balance against my duty—I must go."

With his pen in hand he rose and walked to the window looking out toward the Washington Monument, stood silent for a few seconds, and, as he turned around and looked at me, I saw moisture in his eyes. I paused a moment, and then turning, left the room. There was lead where my heart ought to be, but I knew the debate was closed, that there was nothing I could do except to go with him and take such care of him as I could.

CHAPTER

14

I T WAS ON September 3rd that he started on the mission against which I had so earnestly protested for the sake of his health. For him the journey was a prolonged agony of physical pain; for Mrs. Wilson and me an unceasing agony of anxiety.

During the trip he worked under the most unfavorable conditions. He made speeches daily to record-breaking crowds and shook hands with hundreds of spectators. He was again deprived of exercise, and, in addition, subjected to sudden changes of climate and altitude. The steel cars of the special train held the heat like ovens. There was no question that he needed rest, but he was unable to get enough because of the fast schedule that had to be maintained. The terrific strain which he had been under for more than a year was telling, and his exertions on the western trip were sapping his vitality very fast. With it all he was under enormous emotional strain because he felt that he was fighting the fight of future generations. Again and again as we rode through the crowded streets of western cities he would look intently at the lines of school children on the pavements and say: "I am the attorney for these children."

From the time we reached Montana the President suffered from asthmatic attacks and severe headaches, which seriously interfered with his rest. Frequently I was summoned during the night to give him necessary aid and to assist him in breathing. It was necessary for him to sleep a good part of the time sitting up, propped up with pillows in a chair, but he was so considerate that frequently when an attack would recur, instead of sending for me, he would get up, prop himself up in a chair, and remain there.

The full justification of my fears was realized after he addressed audiences during stops in Denver and Pueblo, Colorado, on September 25th. All day the President had such a splitting headache that, as he expressed it, he could hardly see. Leaving the Pueblo auditorium he went directly back to the train. He was very tired and suffering when he entered the car. I was concerned as to the best method of restoring him so that he could continue the trip, as there were now only five scheduled addresses remaining. I asked the President whether in his opinion it would be of benefit if he could get out and stretch his legs by taking a walk. He agreed and we stopped the special train some twenty miles outside of Pueblo; and the President, Mrs. Wilson, and myself went for a walk. We stepped along at as brisk a pace as was possible without tiring the President too much.

An elderly farmer, who was driving along the road in a small automobile, recognized the President and stopped his car. He asked to have the honor of shaking hands with the President, and after doing this presented him with a head of cabbage and some apples, expressing the hope that the cabbage could be used for dinner that night.

We walked for the better part of an hour. En route back to the train, the President saw a soldier in a private's uniform sitting in a chair on the porch of a house some distance back of the road. He was very plainly ill. Mr. Wilson climbed over the fence and went over and shook hands with him. The boy's father, mother, and brothers came out while the President was talking to him, and were very much touched with the consideration which the President had shown in stopping to express sympathy for the sick youth.

We then returned to the train bringing the apples and the cabbage with us. The trip was resumed for Wichita, Kansas, where the President was scheduled to make an address the following morning. He was very desirous of retiring after dinner to get some rest, but at the first stop, Rocky Ford, Colorado, a large crowd surged about the car and shouted for him to come out and shake hands with them. Secretary Tumulty and others on the train were very anxious that the President should spend the entire time on the platform shaking hands with the people. I did my best to persuade the President to remain inside the car until just before the train pulled out. Then the President came out on the platform and grasped the hands of those who were closest to the rear end of the train. As the train moved out he stood and waved his hand to the people lined up on either side of the tracks, and then returned to his room.

Early the next morning I was awakened from my sleep and told that the President was suffering very much. I went at once and found that he was on the verge of a complete breakdown. His own consciousness of his physical exhaustion helped to make him understand the dire necessity of the situation. But even then there was a flash of his own grim resolution, for he rose and shaved himself as usual, though any other man would have omitted that ceremonial altogether. It was with great difficulty that I could persuade him to turn back to Washington and omit the remainder of the itinerary. He insisted that he must go on saying: "I should feel like a deserter. My opponents will accuse me of having cold feet should I stop now."

I replied: "I owe it to the country, to you, and to your family not to permit you to continue." I told him that if he would try to make another speech he would fall before his audience.

Mrs. Wilson added her pleas to my urgent medical advice, and at last he turned to me and said sadly: "I suppose you are right"; and tears ran down his cheek as he added: "This is the greatest disappointment of my life."

We arrived in Washington on Sunday, the 28th of September, and he walked erect from the station platform to the White House car which was awaiting him. He wanted to go to church that morning but I persuaded him not to do so. In the afternoon, accompanied by Mrs. Wilson and myself, he took a short automobile ride.

In the following three days he consented to rest and to ride out daily. On the evening of October 1st he seemed quite bright and cheerful, played billiards a few minutes, and appeared better than at any time since he started on the western trip. But early the next morning the crash came. He fell stricken with a thrombosis. Mrs. Wilson was never braver, more composed. She and I got him on the bed, and we knew that the giant had fallen. A clot had formed in an artery in the brain, though there was no rupture.

I summoned in consultation Doctor Sterling Ruffin, Rear Admiral E.R. Stitt, and Doctor F.X. Dercum of Philadelphia. Later I called in Doctor H.A. Fowler, Doctor Hugh H. Young, Doctor George De Schweinitz, and Doctor Charles Mayo. At intervals the President's friend and classmate, Doctor E.P. Davis, would confer with me about the case.

CHAPTER

15

HIS BODY WAS BROKEN, but his intellect was unimpaired and his lion spirit untamed. His collapse brought no weakening of his purpose. Foes demanded a compromise covenant in a form which President Wilson believed would draw its teeth. Perhaps he believed that the fight over reservations was only a maneuver, that to comply with the reservationists would merely give opportunity for fresh objections and further mutilation. But, above all, he believed in the covenant as it had been finally agreed upon in Paris, believed that it conformed in its basic principles to the initiatory ideas which he had conceived as essential to a world consort, and he was unwilling to have it tampered with on partisan grounds.

In a remarkable interview with the newspapermen in the Hotel Crillon in Paris on June 27th he had, in reply to a question, said that he had been surprised that he had been able to keep the covenant so close to his original Fourteen Points, and he had, at that time, openly praised Clemenceau and Lloyd George for the manner in which they had coöperated after they had sifted and weighed the purpose of the plan. He was unwilling to yield at home what he had won abroad. He believed that the objections in the Senate were chiefly political and that the representations to the people that the plan was un-American were disingenuous. He proudly craved, for America, leadership in the new order of international dealings.

When he was able to receive visitors, some of his own political supporters called on him to advise compromise, arguing that half a loaf was better than no bread, but one and all left the sick room with renewed admiration for his superb fighting spirit and with fresh resolve to continue the battle on the President's own lines.

He had an important interview with Senator Hitchcock, on the morning of November 17, 1919, who asked him if he had read the Lodge Resolution, and whether he had anything to suggest concerning it. The President immediately replied: "I consider it a nullification of the Treaty and utterly impossible." He then drew an analogy between this and South Carolina's threat to nullify the Constitution. Senator Hitchcock then called the President's attention to the changes the Senate had made in Article X, to which the President replied: "That cuts the very heart out of the Treaty; I could not stand for those changes for a moment because it would humiliate the United States before all of the allied countries."

Senator Hitchcock said: "What would be the effect of the defeat of the Treaty by the Lodge Resolution?"

The President's answer was: "The United States would suffer the contempt of the world. We will be playing into Germany's hands. Think of the humiliation we would suffer in having to ask Germany whether she would accept such and such reservation!" The President said: "If the opponents are bent on defeating this Treaty, I want the vote of each Republican and Democrat recorded, because they will have to answer to the country in the future for their acts. They must answer to the people. I am a sick man, lying in this bed, but I am going to debate this issue with these gentlemen in their respective states whenever they come up for reëlection if I have breath enough in my body to carry on the fight. I shall do this even if I have to give my life to it. And I will get their political scalps when the truth is known to the people. They have got to account to their constituents for their actions in this matter. I have no doubt as to what the verdict of the people will be when they know the facts."

Senator Hitchcock favored certain compromises with the Republicans. The President said: "With the exception of interpretations, which would not alter the substance, I am not willing to make any compromise other than that we have already agreed upon."

The President's position was that he would not oppose reservations which were merely interpretations of the Treaty, but that he was irreconcilably opposed to any alteration of the Treaty which would cause a recommitment to council with other nations.

The Senator told the President that he had had a conference with Lord Grey, the British Ambassador, and with M. Jusserand, the French Ambassador. They told the Senator that they considered that Senator Lodge and the Republican party had killed the Peace Treaty and the League of Nations. They also commented on the fact that this view had been published in both English and French papers. They also expressed the belief that their countries would reject a Treaty amended in accordance with the Lodge Resolution.

The President discussed at length with Senator Hitchcock occurrences connected with the Treaty debate in the Senate, the interview lasting one hour and five minutes. Whenever Senator Hitchcock would bring forth some argument why so and so was done, the President would combat him and ask to be advised why it was done and for what purpose. He said repeatedly: "Senator, I think you have acted very wisely and used good judgment in the circumstances, but why did you do so and so? I am not criticising you, but I am asking you for information."

As the interview was drawing to a close the President said: "If it is not too much trouble, will you please send me a little notice of what is transpiring during the day so that at your next visit we may discuss the situation?" The Senator replied that he would be very glad to comply with his request.

As the Senator arose to leave the room, he said: "Mr. President, I hope I have not weakened you by this long discussion."

And the President smiling replied: "No, Senator, you have strengthened me against the opponents."

After the Senator and I had left the room, the Senator turned to me and said: "The President is looking remarkably well. He has strengthened so much more since I saw him last. He is very combative today as he sits up there in that bed. On certain compromises he is as immovable as the Rock of Gibraltar." The Senator also said to me: "I would give anything if the Senate could see the attitude that man took this morning. Think how effective it would be if they could see the picture as you and I saw it!"

Mr. Wilson's confidence in the rightness of his ideas and his faith that the people would see the wisdom of the new order which he advocated made it unbelievable to him that the Senate could dare to reject the measure. All this accorded with his normal habit of looking far ahead. He foresaw that without America's responsible participation in world affairs, Europe would collapse and that sooner or later America must be drawn into the whirlpool.

He never failed to rise to an occasion. Only once

did I see him when he seemed temporarily beaten in spirit. That was after the Senate rejected the Treaty of Versailles by a vote of 49 to 35 on March 19, 1920. The President had never believed this action possible. All his instinct of right and the triumph of right were opposed to it. When he heard the news he sighed deeply and said: "I feel like going to bed and staying there." That night was a very restless one for him. He was doing a lot of thinking but holding his tongue. I was with him in his bedroom several times during the night. At about three o'clock he turned to me and said: "Doctor, the devil is a busy man." This is all he said. Later he summoned me. "Doctor, please get the Bible there and read from Second Corinthians, Chapter 4, Verses 8 and 9."

Finding the passage I read:

We are troubled on every side, yet not distressed; *we are* perplexed, but not in despair;
Persecuted, but not forsaken; cast down, but not destroyed . . .

He said: "If I were not a Christian, I think I should go mad, but my faith in God holds me to the belief that He is in some way working out His own plans through human perversities and mistakes."

Another March day when I said to him: "Good morning, it is a beautiful spring day and warm"; he replied: "I don't know whether it is warm or cold. I feel so weak and useless. I feel that I would like to go back to bed and stay there until I either get well or die. I cannot make a move to do my work except by making a definite resolve to do so." He said further that the League of Nations "is the birth of the spirit of the times," and that "those who oppose it will be gibbeted and occupy an unenviable position in history along with Benedict Arnold and Gates."

CHAPTER

16

THE PRESIDENT RETAINED his sense of humor in desperate illness in an extraordinary way. After he was stricken in the White House he met me every day with a joke when I would go in to see him. On October 11th he was extremely ill and weak and even to speak was an exertion. He had difficulty in swallowing. He was being given liquid nourishment and frequently it took a good deal of persuasion to get him to take even this simple diet. Mrs. Wilson and I were begging him to take this nourishment, and, after taking a number of mouthfuls given to him by Mrs. Wilson with a spoon, he held up one finger and motioned me to come nearer. He said to me in a whisper: "Doctor, I must repeat to you this limerick:

> A wonderful bird is the pelican
> His bill will hold more than his bellican.
> He can take in his beak enough food for a week
> I wonder how in the hell-he-can.

Another day as I turned a light on his eyes he asked

me what I was up to and I said: "I am examining your pupils."

To which he replied: "You have a large order, as I have had a great many in my day."

He was fond, in health and illness alike, of referring to his teaching days and to his students. He once remarked that among the best reports he got from abroad were those from Roland S. Morris, Ambassador to Japan, and when I asked him how he accounted for this superiority of Mr. Morris' documents, he replied jokingly: "That's easy. Because he was a pupil of mine at Princeton."

He always showed during his extreme illness an active interest in my manipulations of him. For instance, once when I was percussing his chest, he said: "Why knock? I am at home." The President did not have a shave from October 2nd until November 12th, and his beard had grown to a considerable length. At one time Dr. Hugh Young was in consultation in the President's room, and I remarked to him: "Don't you think the President would feel more comfortable if he had his beard cut off?"

Dr. Young agreed and said, "Could you shave him? You know, in the olden days the doctors were barbers." And he went on to say that the colors, red and white, on the barber's sign represented the red blood on the white skin. He added: "And doctors were really barbers in those days."

The President looking up at us said: "And they are barbarous yet."

Once after he had been able to leave his bed and walk with the assistance of his cane he was crossing a rug with a number of figures woven in it, such as the Washington Monument, the Capitol, and Niagara Falls. As the President crossed the rug he turned to me and said: "Doctor, that is not a bad stunt for a lame fellow, to walk over Niagara Falls this morning."

Even in the final illness, while death was stealing on him, he joked. I had called into consultation Dr. Ruffin and Dr. Fowler. While they were waiting outside the sickroom I told Mr. Wilson that I had two other doctors whom I wished to see him. With a feeble smile he said: "Be careful. Too many cooks spoil the broth." That was Woodrow Wilson's last jest.

His sense of humor was a lieutenant to his imperious will in carrying him through the struggles and the sufferings of the war experience and the aftermath. It stood by him in the grimmest moments of the war, and it was with him when he died.

CHAPTER

17

Principle always counted for more with Mr. Wilson
than any personality, even his own. He was not happy
in bitter fighting. If he hurt others, he also hurt himself, but he could not spare anybody's feelings, not
even his own, where principles were involved. As I
was daily, almost hourly, present during his illness in
the White House, I have many recollections of the
way his mind was working on matters small and great.

I was called into the President's room at two o'clock
on the morning of April 13, 1920. He was awake when
I entered the room. I sat by his bedside and he talked
for about two hours. Among the things he said was
this: "When I get out of office and my health has re-
covered I want to devote a good deal of time to showing what a disorganization the United States Senate
is." He went on to explain the "double-dealing of
some of the Senators," referring particularly to Senators Hoke Smith, James A. Reed, and Henry Cabot
Lodge. He said that he had asked our boys to go over-

seas and to fight in the trenches for a principle—and for this principle many of them gave up their lives and many were wounded. Now these men in the Senate took away all this from our soldiers. He asked: "Could any self-respecting man ask our boys to go into another war? Could you expect them to make such a sacrifice, and then have a crowd in the Senate like this throw away what they had fought for?"

During the conversation he said: "I am seriously thinking what is my duty to the country on account of my physical condition. My personal pride must not be allowed to stand in the way of my duty to the country. If I am only half efficient I should turn the office over to the Vice-President. If it is going to take much time for me to recover my health and strength, the country cannot afford to wait for me." He asked: "What do you think?"

I reviewed to him all that he was doing and how he was keeping in touch with the affairs of the Government and conducting its business. It was here that I persuaded him to hold a Cabinet meeting.

I said: "If you will call a Cabinet meeting and come in contact with your advisers in a body—thus far you have been conferring with them individually—and talk with them, you can then determine just what your leadership represents. If you will do this I am confident that you will find that you are accomplishing more than you realize; and it will reassure you of your ability to continue to handle the situation."

The President said: "I have had nothing but discouragement from those who should support me and should coöperate with me and stand for the principles for which I stand. I have stood for principles and not for personalities; many have failed me in this crucial time. If I were well and strong I would gladly and eagerly fight for the cause stronger than ever. I will try not to be discouraged even as it is, and I shall make the best of the circumstances."

The President, on April 14th, held the first Cabinet meeting since his illness. The meeting was held at 10:00 o'clock in the White House study. He enjoyed meeting with the various members of the Cabinet and talking with them. I suggested beforehand that it last only an hour to prevent him from overtaxing himself, and that I come in at the end of an hour. This would be the signal for the adjournment of the meeting. When I entered the room, according to our prearranged plan, he shook his head at me, meaning that I should not interrupt them. At the end of an hour and fifteen minutes I again entered the room, with the same result. At 11:30 I returned with Mrs. Wilson, and he then reluctantly adjourned the meeting. He showed very plainly that it had done him a lot of good. When I asked him if he wanted to give anything to the press about the Cabinet meeting, he said: "No, I do not believe so."

I said, "Won't some of the Cabinet members give out what transpired?"

He replied: "I do not know. I doubt if they will."
He then added: "Lane was the leak of the Cabinet
when he was a member."

One night he summoned me to his room, and asking the nurse to leave us, he said: "I have been thinking over this matter of resigning and letting the Vice-
President take my place. It is clear that I should do
this if I have not the strength to fill the office. If I
become convinced that the country is suffering any
ill effects from my sickness I shall summon Congress
in special session and have you arrange to get me
wheeled in my chair into the House of Representatives. I shall have my address of resignation prepared
and shall try to read it myself, but if my voice is not
strong enough I shall ask the Speaker of the House to
read it, and at its conclusion I shall be wheeled out
of the room."

As he never broached this topic again, it is evident
that he believed what was true, that he had the
strength to administer the office capably.

The first talk he had with me on the subject of the
League of Nations since the defeat of the treaty in the
Senate took place on the morning of March 25th.
While seated at his desk in his study in the White
House the President said to me: "I note from the
papers that members of the House and of the Senate
are speculating as to what steps I will take relative to
the defeat of the Peace Treaty. They are wondering
whether I will veto a resolution declaring peace with

Germany, in case they pass such a resolution, or whether I am going to write a message. My present intention is to do nothing. If they pass a resolution declaring peace with Germany, I will then express my views in a message—which I know will be extremely distasteful to the Senate. I do not doubt but that they may try to impeach me for it. If I were well and on my feet and they pursued such a course, I would gladly accept the challenge, because I could put them in such a light before the country that I believe the people would impeach them. I do not think that in the history of the country, the Senate was ever as unpopular with the people as it is now. It would only be necessary for the people to understand the facts in order to impeach them. The time for the San Francisco and Chicago Conventions is near at hand and the referendum can be determined there preparatory to going before the people.

"I have done all in my power to get this Treaty through as it originally stood. My sole purpose was to see that it was not torn up or emasculated so that it would not stand the test of time. I entered into that Treaty under solemn obligations with our Allies. We each promised, after much giving and taking, to stand by what we had formulated, and for me now to go back on that promise by changing or by permitting a change of the substance of the Treaty would be to break faith with my colleagues. I would feel were I to violate my promise that I could never give them an honest look in the face again."

The President continued. "Tumulty has sent me a letter asking that I come out and say that I will not run again for the Presidency. I do not see anything to be gained at this time by doing so except to turn the leadership of the Democratic Party over to William Jennings Bryan. In my opinion this would be a pretty state of affairs for the country and for the world at this stage of world conditions. I feel that it would be presumptuous and in bad taste for me to decline something that has not been offered to me. No group of men has given me any assurances that it wanted me to be a candidate for renomination. In fact, everyone seems to be opposed to my running. And I think it would be entirely out of place for me to say now that I would not run. With things in such a turmoil in the United States and throughout the world as they are today, the Democratic Convention in San Francisco may get into a hopeless tie-up, and it may, by the time of the Convention, become imperative that the League of Nations and the Peace Treaty be made the dominant issue. The Convention may come to a deadlock as to candidates, and there may be practically a universal demand for the selection of someone to lead them out of the wilderness. The members of the Convention may feel that I am the logical one to lead—perhaps the only one to champion this cause. In such circumstances I would feel obliged to accept the nomination even if I thought it would cost me my life. I have given my vitality, and almost my life, for the League of Nations, and I would rather lead a fight for the League of Nations and lose both my reputation and my life than shirk a duty of this kind if it is absolutely necessary for me to make the fight and if there is no one else to do it. Certain politicians in both parties are guessing as to what will be my future course. I think it is the best thing for the world to keep them guessing for the present at any rate. I see nothing to be gained by making a declaration that I will not run, especially since I have not been asked to be a candidate by anyone."

The President did all the talking on this occasion. He did not ask me if I thought he could stand another Presidential campaign, and, for medical reasons, I preferred not to volunteer any advice. I did not want to tell him that it would be impossible for him to take part in such a campaign, as I was fearful that it might have a depressing effect upon him.

While I was sitting with him in his bedroom before an open wood fire on the evening of May 2, 1920, the President remarked about the future of the world. "Upon the President elected this fall depends whether the United States will be the leader of the world or back among the stragglers." He added that the League of Nations and the Peace Treaty are bigger than any party, but he did not know whom he would pick for President now if he had the choosing.

The President had a restless night July 1st and

called me at 3 A.M. "Doctor, please examine my lungs.
They feel as if they have no air in them." I sat by the
bedside and talked until 3:45. We discussed the pros
and cons for the Democratic nomination and the
President said he was much gratified over the Convention proceedings so far. A day or two later the
President became concerned over the balloting in the
Convention. There had been twenty-two ballots and
no selection with Cox, McAdoo, and Palmer leading
but in a deadlock. I sat up until 3 A.M. July 3rd at
the Executive Office with Tumulty and others. I then
visited the President to give him the results of the
ballots. He made no comments except, "if they nominate Cox, he is one of the weakest of the lot."

A couple of weeks later the Democratic nominees,
Governor Cox and Franklin D. Roosevelt, met with
the President on the rear portico of the White House.
The President greeted Governor Cox: "I am sincerely
glad to see you and to congratulate you." They discussed the San Francisco Convention, the issues of the
campaign, the League of Nations, and the President
told many stories.

At lunch with the President and Mrs. Wilson were
Cox, Roosevelt, Senator Glass, Tumulty, J.R. Bolling,
and myself. After lunch, Cox, Roosevelt, and I walked
down to the basement floor on the way to the Executive Office. As we reached the kitchen door, Swem,
the President's stenographer, appeared with the Presi-

dent's statement which he then read from his shorthand notes. Cox listened most attentively. "That is fine."

The President had dictated this statement so quickly that Swem was able to overtake us on the way to the Executive Office. Early the next morning when I was called to the President's room to relieve an asthmatic spell, the President remarked: "Cox is a fine fellow."

His faith in the people made him confident of a Democratic victory in 1920. When others foresaw that postwar reactions and discontents must result in Republican success at the polls, he called them pessimists and kept serene faith in the triumph of what he believed was right.

After the overwhelming defeat he read in the newspaper that Governor Cox had stated that he planned to visit the devastated regions of France. The President smiled a little and grimly said: "Why go so far to see devastation?"

The day after the election, which Republican leaders and newspapers acclaimed as defeat of Wilsonism (Governor Cox, the candidate, had strongly supported the League of Nations in his campaign but was a secondary figure to the old warrior in the White House), Mr. and Mrs. Wilson rode out as if nothing had happened. Whether acclaimed or rejected he was the same. No words can fit him so well as those lines of

Wordsworth's "Character of the Happy Warrior," one
of Mr. Wilson's favorite poems:

> Who, whether praise of him must walk the earth
> For ever, and to noble deeds give birth,
> Or he must fall, to sleep without his fame,
> And leave a dead unprofitable name—
> Finds comfort in himself and in his cause;
> And, while the mortal mist is gathering, draws
> His breath in confidence of Heaven's applause . . .

CHAPTER

18

HE SERVED OUT the remainder of his term with his customary strict interpretation of his duty, and insisted on playing his last public act as if he were in his normal health. He performed with decorum the concluding duties, ceremonials, and courtesies of the great office which he was laying down after eight years crowded with stupendous events. He insisted that he would ride with Mr. Harding to the Capitol, sign papers, and accompany the President-elect to the inauguration platform in the usual manner.

I visited the Capitol and carefully surveyed the situation. I saw that in order to reach the inaugural platform he would have to climb steep, long stairways, which was practically impossible for him. Then when I stated the case to him, he at first protested but the next morning said that he would comply with my judgment and not attend the ceremonies on the inaugural platform.

He carried out this program with grave courtesy.

Mr. Harding, in turn, was attentive and considerate. None who saw the two figures that day could have guessed that the stalwart, active, middle-aged President-elect, who appeared younger than his years, would die before his companion, who in two years had grown to be an old man. Both died in less than three years from that day.

The two chatted together pleasantly before the formal march up the Avenue began. Mr. Harding, remarking on his love for pet animals, said that some day he hoped to own a domesticated elephant, to which Mr. Wilson replied that he hoped it would not prove to be a white elephant.

On the drive to the Capitol, Mr. Wilson insisted that the cheering was for the new President and therefore looked straight ahead without bowing any acknowledgments. In view of the demonstration which Mr. Wilson received when he rode in the procession in honor of the Unknown Soldier eight months later, it may be questioned whether his views were correct about the cheering on March 4, 1921. There was mingled applause for both men and enough to go around.

On arrival at the Capitol, Mr. Wilson went directly to the President's room to sign bills. Senator Lodge, in his official capacity, advanced and informed him that the Senate awaited his further directions. Mr. Wilson stated that there was nothing more, and said, "Good morning, sir."

Presently a clock boomed twelve. It was a sign that

the Administration had changed, that President Warren G. Harding had succeeded to office, and that President Wilson was now Mr. Wilson, a private citizen.

There was a general movement to the Senate Chamber, where the Vice-President was to be inaugurated, and Mr. and Mrs. Wilson, Secretary Tumulty, and I were left alone with one secret service man. After descending in the elevator to the ground level, Mr. Wilson limped slowly to his car with the aid of his cane. He and Mrs. Wilson and I drove to the modest home which he had purchased in S Street, a house destined for the next three years to be almost as much a goal for sightseers as the White House itself.

Our route from the Capitol to the new home was through New Jersey Avenue and Massachusetts Avenue. These thoroughfares were as silent and deserted as on an early Sunday morning. It was as if the entire population had flocked to the Capitol. We drove in silence; and I reflected on the contrast between this scene and the noise and glamour of the ride up Pennsylvania Avenue some two hours before, and the great cheering throngs along the Paris boulevards and in London and in Rome and in Brussels and in New York on his return from abroad, and I wondered if the thought of the contrast was also passing through his mind. But he gave no sign of what he was thinking.

Soon after we reached the house, where we found many flowers which had been sent to greet him, some of his close friends began to drop in to pay their respects. He talked with them cheerily and assured them that he intended to give to the country an example of the way a former President should conduct himself. The years that followed showed what he meant. There was never an open word of criticism of the Harding Administration, and he maintained consistent public silence except in the Armistice Day addresses, in which he summoned his fellow-countrymen to remember the great cause for which the war had been fought.

Once, for instance, when I was quoting something derogatory to President Harding, Mr. Wilson said: "No, we mustn't criticize President Harding, because we don't know the facts as he knows them, and we don't know whether or not a revelation of the facts might be harmful to the public interests. I myself have had enough experience of that kind of injustice based on the ignorance of my critics to feel a sympathy for President Harding, though I am not of his political faith and he would in no circumstance have been my choice for the Presidency."

There was a heavy private correspondence from which an occasional letter would get into print, but never with his connivance. He held it his privilege to write unfavorably about Democratic Senators who had aided in obstructing the passage of the treaty, but these opinions were expressed in reply to direct questions from personal correspondents.

Fighting for a principle was a religion for him. He was as sensitive as a poet, at times supersensitive, and yet he must keep fighting for those things in which he believed, though the fighting should lead to the alienation of personal friends and to the crucifixion of some of his strongest affections.

On April 5, 1922, Mr. Tumulty wrote a letter to Mr. Wilson asking that he give him a statement to take to New York to be read at the Jefferson Day banquet where James M. Cox would be one of the principal speakers. Mr. Wilson replied that he thought it would be unwise for him to give out a statement to be read at the dinner especially since it was his present policy not to give out statements on public questions. A few days later Tumulty wrote Mr. Wilson a long letter begging him to reconsider; but Mr. Wilson replied that for him to give a letter that would appear to endorse Cox would be construed as an endorsement for Cox's renomination in 1924, and he would consider Cox's renomination as the suicide of the Democratic Party. However, Tumulty did convey a message at the banquet purportedly from Mr. Wilson.

Mr. Wilson seemed much distressed and pained to write a letter to the New York *Times* about the Tumulty incident, but he said it was a question of personal privilege; that he could not let it go unanswered. He felt that it had to be answered through the papers to correct the wrong impression which had been given out. He said that he hated to do this to Tumulty, but if it had been his son he would have had to act in the same manner.

A few days after the publication of the letter I expressed regret that he had broken with **Tumulty, as** his enemies would be sure to say that he could not get along with anyone. He abruptly told me that I did not know what I was talking about; that it was none of my business. Several days after this conversation, while in bed, he asked Mrs. Wilson and the colored attendant to please step out of the room as he wanted to talk over some private matters with me. After they had left the room, he said: "I want to apologize for the way in which I spoke to you the other day. I want you to read these letters which will explain the whole situation."

CHAPTER

19

THE THOUGHT THAT HE, by recommending to Congress a declaration of war, had sent the flower of American youth to the trenches, the field of battle, and the military camps, made the soldiers especially dear to him. He could seldom refer to them without emotion. He believed that they fought for the greatest cause of battle that the world has ever known, and he believed that they constituted the greatest army in the history of warfare. They were his "comrades."

After the termination of his Presidency, much of his voluminous correspondence was with former servicemen, particularly the invalided. Between him and them there was a mutual recognition of comradeship —they had been broken in the same cause. Some of them wrote him charmingly naïve letters, badly spelled, atrociously "slangy"—sometimes there was doggerel verse in the letters, ranging in theme from "Old Glory" to "cooties"—one of the latter inspirations described the cootie in terms of affection, as "one that sticketh closer than a brother." One of the war stories that Mr. Wilson loved was about a doughboy who stooped down in the trench to remove a biting cootie from his leg; at that instant a "whiz-bang" passed over his head and exploded. Stooping had saved his life. The cootie had caused him to stoop, so he took the cootie from the ground and put it back on his leg—the insect had earned the right to continue its meal!

In his automobile rides around Washington he seemed to have an intuition for the presence of the uniform of a soldier, sailor, or marine, and would salute every service or ex-serviceman he passed, often when he was not recognized by the young men themselves.

A wounded soldier on the roadside was always a signal for the chauffeur to stop the car. There was many a chat between Mr. Wilson and the men. Some of the encounters were pathetic, some humorous. He had a meeting over in Virginia with Angus McGregor about which he would tell with gusto, for Angus was an upstanding fellow, even though he couldn't stand at all, but had to swing himself along on his crutches, his shattered feet merely brushing the ground. Angus had been an aviator, and was brought down over the lines by a German plane. "He got me, but I got him too," said Angus, "and by dropping him and his plane I saved the lives of a lot of our fellows for he was out to bomb our trenches." Of course, Mr. Wilson liked that, liked also the indomitable optimism of Angus.

It was on a Sunday afternoon, December, 1921, that they met. Mr. Wilson's classmate, Cleveland Dodge, was spending the day with him—a happy day for Mr. Wilson, who bubbled with laughter and anecdote in the warming presence of this beloved friend. After lunch Mr. and Mrs. Wilson and Mr. and Mrs. Dodge went for a ride in Virginia. At the rickety old bridge which crossed Hunting Creek, they got their first sight of Angus McGregor, swinging himself along by his shoulders and his crutches. Of course the car stopped, and Angus was bidden to get in, which he did with the assistance of Mr. Dodge. Angus talked freely. He was on his way back home to Suffolk—two hundred miles away.

"Surely not afoot!" Mr. Wilson exclaimed—if Angus' mode of locomotion could be called "afoot." Well, Angus "expected" people would give him lifts along the way, people were "mighty good about that." He had spent all his money getting to Washington to see his sister, but had arrived only to find that she had closed up the house and gone to Suffolk. So he had turned around and was on his way back.

Mr. Dodge, who had joined in the conversation, ranging wide over Angus' war and hospital experience, told Angus that he wanted to pay his railway fare back to Suffolk. Angus said he couldn't take the money unless Mr. Dodge would give him his address so he could return it. "Oh," said Mr. Dodge, "never mind the address; I am just an old gray Santa Claus;

if you must regard the money as a loan, pass it on to some other soldier in need of a lift."

Before Angus left them to take the train, Mr. Wilson requested that he write to him and tell him how he fared on the journey. In due time the letter arrived. It was from the Jefferson Hotel in Richmond. That was probably like Angus, the blessed optimist. Penniless on the roadside one day, the next day a guest at the Jefferson. Angus will always encounter Santa Claus somewhere. He deserves to. And he will be Santa Claus to the other fellow if he has any money, as Angus would probably say, "in his jeans." Mr. Wilson loved Angus and remembered him.

When Mrs. Wilson told the story of Angus to Mr. and Mrs. Charles Dana Gibson, Mrs. Gibson exclaimed: "Fancy being picked up on the road by Woodrow Wilson and Cleveland Dodge! It was worth being smashed up for."

But Angus was only one of a multitude of soldier friends that Mr. Wilson acquired in his days of relaxation after leaving the White House.

CHAPTER

20

I CONTINUED to be Mr. Wilson's physician, and I am proud to say his friend, after he moved into S Street. Being continually in and out of the house I saw him in all his moods and had many long and confidential talks with him. At times he would be depressed and I would seek the cause to find the remedy. Sometimes the cause was physical, sometimes it was distress of mind over the drift of public affairs, and he would express opinions of men and measures which I am not at liberty to divulge. Sometimes he was his old jocose self, would relate a new anecdote, or say: "I have a new limerick for you."

In referring to the practice of designating certain weeks for specific movements—such as, Be Kind to Animals Week, Clean Up Week, Music Week, National Air Week, Better Homes Week—he said there should be a week designated for people to mind their own business.

If in some ways he grew more severe as he grew older, in other ways he grew more tender. He had more "moods," or at least indulged them more, after his illness began. High-strung and intense of nature, ill, broken in nerves, it would have been strange if he had not sometimes been caustic and impatient and severe. But at other times, and quite as frequently, he would be tender as a child, sympathetic as a woman, and sometimes with a kindness that radiated to all around him.

To see him in one of those moods of sunshine was to see a lovely and memorable spectacle. Seated in the library in S Street, always in the same chair, in exactly the same nook by the fireplace, he would turn on everybody in the room in rotation a face that shone with loving kindness, a face that seemed more placid after the expressions of pain and severe thought had passed from it.

In these latter days he was less calculable than in the early days, but his moods in the latter days were not less winning than of old—only different. His long, hard battles for the things in which he believed changed him in some ways on the surface, but in the depths of him there was something unchanged. The sunshine was still there, though at times it might be temporarily concealed by clouds of sorrow, pain, and grim purpose. It would be obviously unfair for a visitor to report sharp things said by Mr. Wilson in his nervous irritability without testifying to the sweetness and nobility that remained unmodified.

It was on the afternoon of Thursday, December 28,

1922—Mr. Wilson's sixty-sixth birthday anniversary —that I dropped in at S Street to wish him many happy returns of the day. I called at two o'clock and spent an hour with him. He was in better spirits and looked better than he had since his great illness. There was a healthy glow to his skin and he spoke with animation. He was dressed in anticipation of meeting a delegation representing the Woodrow Wilson Foundation, which called on him at three o'clock.

Mr. Wilson was seated in what he called his "old Princeton Chair." It is a plain, wooden chair, with arms, and with a high back. The seat is of brown leather with the arms also mounted in brown leather. The black paint is worn off at places where his elbows have rubbed. It is not a revolving chair. He spoke very affectionately of his old chair, saying: "This chair stood by me through all my days at Princeton; we have encountered stormy weather." He also had his old Princeton desk in his bedroom—a flat-top desk, with drawers at the sides, and in these he kept his private papers. He used this desk constantly while at Princeton.

On this afternoon he took delight in showing me through the library and dining room, calling my attention to the large number of beautiful bouquets and baskets of flowers that had been sent to him by admiring friends on this natal day. "It is very pleasing to be remembered by my friends in this way," he said. He then pointed to a large pile of cards with all sorts of felicitous remarks indicated on them. There was quite a basketful of these cards which had been left during the day. He said: "I am having quite a card party today, as you see."

He also called my attention to the large number of letters and telegrams on his desk—perhaps the largest mail he had received on any one day in S Street. He made no comment, simply pointed to the pile. He did refer, however, to one letter which he had received that morning and which was signed by a number of World War veterans, which read in part: "You have been wronged, and, by God, we are going to right it"; and as he said this he pounded the arm of his chair with his fist. "That tone and meaning is in nearly every letter that I get from an ex-soldier."

I told him about the Senate Resolution which was adopted unanimously on this day, and which is contained in the following clipping from the *Congressional Record:*

> Whereas the Senate has heard with great pleasure the announcement of the rapid recovery to good health of former President Hon. Woodrow Wilson: Be it
>
> *Resolved,* that the Vice President be requested to express to Hon. Woodrow Wilson the pleasure and joy of the Senate of the United States because of his rapid recovery to good health.

He chuckled and said: "Think of them passing it and not meaning it. Of course, I do not mean to say that all who voted for it were not sincere, for I know many were sincere but I feel sure some of them were not. I would much rather have had three Senators get together and draw up a resolution and have it passed with sincerity than the one that was passed today. That would be worth far more than the one the Senate did pass."

He then repeated this limerick:

> There was an old man of Khartoum, who kept
> two black sheep in his room,
> To remind him, he said, of two friends who were
> dead, but he never would specify whom.

He asked me if by any chance I had read the article in the *Saturday Evening Post* by Dr. John H. Richards, one of Theodore Roosevelt's physicians in his last illness. It appeared in the issue of December 9, 1922, and the particular reference is as follows:

> As Christmas approached, Colonel Roosevelt improved noticeably. He was sitting fully dressed in a chair one morning when I entered the room, and was in rare good humor at the prospect of going home to Sagamore Hill within a few days. I asked him how he was feeling.
> "If this left wrist were a little bit better," he remarked with slow unction, "I would like to be left alone in this room with our great and good President for about fifteen minutes, and then I would cheerfully be hung."

Mr. Wilson said: "Think of a statement of that kind coming from an ex-President. Just think of that."

His tone was by no means bitter, and this is all he said about the article.

President Harding's death was a shock to him. The courtesies had been maintained between the former President and the President, though, of course, they saw nothing of each other personally and held different political views; but when Mrs. Harding was seriously ill Mr. and Mrs. Wilson called and left their cards. President Harding was touched by this, said it was a wonderful thing for a sick man of the opposition party to call in person to express his sympathies. It is said that after President Harding's death Mr. Wilson's card was found preserved in the flap of the blotter on the President's desk.

On a day of intense heat many months later Mr. Wilson attended President Harding's funeral as a sincere mourner. His desire to participate in the exercises was conveyed in a note in which he requested that his "friend, Admiral Grayson" be permitted to accompany him and Mrs. Wilson.

According to his custom we were prompt to the minute in arriving at the White House and sat for nearly an hour under a killing sun, which was prostrating stalwart Marines in their full-dress uniforms. But he sat calmly, patiently, gravely. His equanimity was ruffled only once when a Colonel, whose own head must have been turned by the heat, rushed up and asked excitedly: "Mr. Wilson, may I ask you a question?"

Mr. Wilson answered: "Certainly."

"Could you tell me whether Senator Lodge has arrived or not?"

Mr. Wilson replied: "I can not." And then asked me what asylum that Colonel had escaped from.

CHAPTER

21

Aᴏᴛᴇʀ ʜᴇ ᴛᴏᴏᴋ ᴜᴘ residence in S Street until the summer of 1923, there was a slow improvement in his condition, no marked change from week to week, but a gratifying change when his case was reviewed over the period of months. The chart showed a general improvement. The muscles of the affected left side grew stronger. However, there were complications which caused me anxiety at times, and there were setbacks from which he would rally, and after which he would be stronger than he had been before. He was game and tried to take advantage of each upward step. There was, however, a general arteriosclerosis, which, of course, made final recovery impossible.

In the autumn of 1923 his good eye began to fail; there were minute hemorrhages in the retina. Though he kept his courage and was frequently as cheerful as he had ever been, he became increasingly depressed as he discovered that he had difficulty in recognizing people on the street from his motor car, as well as great difficulty in reading, and that new glasses did not remedy the difficulty. This was a sign of progressive arteriosclerosis.

On January 31, 1924, there came a sudden turn for the worse. His stomach ceased to function and the kidneys were involved. Contrary to popular impression, he did not have a second stroke of paralysis. He said to me in one of his last articulate sentences: "The machinery is worn out," adding those words which expressed his religious faith and confidence, "I am ready."

He lingered for two and a half days, his heart muscle growing gradually weaker. He retained consciousness until some twelve or fifteen hours before his death, after which he was intermittently unconscious. His devoted wife was at his bedside through all the day and at intervals throughout the night. The only daughter who was able to reach him before his death was Miss Margaret; Mr. and Mrs. McAdoo not arriving from California until after he had passed away, Mr. and Mrs. Sayre being in Siam. Of course, I spent the entire time at the house and had two trained nurses in attendance and the faithful Scott, the colored man who had been with him ever since he moved into his private home. At 11:15, Sunday morning, February 3rd, he died without struggle, his wife and daughter on one side of the bed, I on the other holding his pulse, and at the foot of the bed two nurses.

I repeat what has been said thousands of times, that he was as much a casualty of the war as any soldier who fell in the field. His death was a result of his consecration to the service of his country and humanity.

At President Harding's funeral Mr. Wilson had expressed a wish for a private funeral for himself. On another occasion, when he and Mrs. Wilson were driving through Arlington, which he loved (the tomb of the Unknown Soldier was especially sacred to him), he had said to his wife that he did not feel he could rest easily in Arlington. Perhaps he who loved quiet places objected to the idea of lying amid tombs of ceremonial pomp. At any rate, Mrs. Wilson had two of his negative wishes to direct her final decisions as to the place of his burial and the character of the funeral. She thought of Staunton, his birthplace, but there was none of his own flesh and blood buried there. She thought of the cemetery in Columbia, South Carolina, where his father and mother were buried, but when President Wilson had interred his sister, Mrs. Howe, in the family plot he had observed that the last space was filled. Finally, in counsel with Bishop Freeman and others she decided on at least a temporary interment in the crypt of the Cathedral of St. Peter and St. Paul on Mount Saint Alban in Washington.

Because his greatest work had been done in Washington and because he had selected the Capital City as his home, it seemed to Mrs. Wilson fitting that he should rest here. Her wish, like his, was for a private funeral. A few intimate friends and members of the family were at the house, where a simple service was conducted by Bishop Freeman, Doctor James H. Taylor, pastor of the Central Presbyterian Church where Mr. Wilson had worshiped, and the Reverend Doctor Sylvester Beach, Mr. Wilson's Princeton pastor. Among the honorary pallbearers were some of his intimate friends of old days and more recent times, some of his Princeton classmates, the physicians who had attended him in his latter illness, and some of his more intimate political associates.

The funeral procession passed slowly between a long double line of mourners extending from the house to the Cathedral door. They were representatives of the great public; some of them had come from a distance—there was no room for them either in the house or in the small cathedral chapel—all they could do was to stand and watch the hearse which bore the nation's fallen leader pass. Funerals of great statesmen and great leaders are sometimes viewed as spectacles. In this throng, on either side of the roadway, there seemed to be no suggestion of mere curiosity in any face; there was sorrow, love, admiration, and here and there was one quietly weeping.

The cathedral chapel was crowded. President Coolidge and his wife were there and so were the members of the Cabinet, the Ambassadors and Ministers from foreign lands, many delegations of representative organizations throughout the land, and a group of his old associates from Princeton. Had the cathedral been completed it could have been filled over and over again many times. As it was, the comparatively small space compelled the exclusion of thousands who wished to be there.

The ceremony in the cathedral was simple and dignified. Bishop Freeman read the service. At the conclusion of the services the President and Mrs. Coolidge left the building, followed by all except the immediate funeral party. Then Bishop Freeman committed the body to the vault and concluded the service by reading Tennyson's, "Crossing the Bar."

I have given a few glimpses of the human side of Woodrow Wilson. All who really knew him, knew how human he was. No man knew this side of him better than I, whose association with him was constant and intimate during the last eleven years and the greatest years of his life. I saw his kindness as well as his strength, his unyielding will, his scorn of weakness and double-dealing, and I knew the lighter side of his nature—the playfulness of his mind and his keen sense of the ludicrous. It has not been easy to suggest the many phases of his nature in a brief sketch. I have given only hints and foreshadowings, for I do not think that the time is ripe for a full-length picture of him.

A final word about a phase of Mr. Wilson which was often misinterpreted—his austerity—what men called his "aloofness."

Mr. Wilson knew how to keep his own counsel, to think when he did not wish to speak. Often we have ridden together for a stretch of miles without exchanging a word. He might break silence to comment briefly, humorously, or sympathetically upon a passing object—a human figure, a child at play, a street sign—and then he would relapse into silence. No one could have been his companion who did not respect his silences as well as his confidences.

There was a sense in which he lived apart and aloft. He could come down from the heights to mingle with other men, to discuss with them state policies, to laugh and chaff with them, but by nature his mind and spirit sought the high spaces—and high spaces are not populous. It is symbolic of his career that his body should lie on Mount Saint Alban, the highest spot in the Capital City of the land.

But it is only the body that lies there, the worn-out machinery, as he described it to me in his last connected sentence. His spirit cannot die. It will survive to guide and direct generations yet unborn. It will survive the hot debates which seem so important today and are so forgotten tomorrow.